UK AIRLINES

Alan J. Wright

IAN ALLAN
Publishing

First Published 1998

ISBN 0 7110 2573 8

All rights reserved. No part of this book may be reproduced or transmitted in any form or by any means, electronic or mechanical, including photocopying, recording or by any information storage and retrieval system, without permission from the Publisher in writing.

© Ian Allan Publishing Ltd 1998

Published by Ian Allan Publishing

an imprint of Ian Allan Publishing Ltd, Terminal House, Station Approach, Shepperton, Surrey TW17 8AS.
Printed by Ian Allan Printing Ltd at its works at Riverdene, Molesey Road, Hersham, Surrey KT12 4RG.

Code: 9806/C2

Front cover:
G-MONB — Boeing 757-2T7 (ER) of Monarch Airlines.
Austin J. Brown/Aviation Picture Library

Back cover:
G-RMCT — Short SD3-60 Varient 100 of Gill Airways.

Title page:
G-IOII — Lockheed L1011 TriStar 100 of Classic Airways.

Picture Credits:
All photographs are by the author unless otherwise credited.

AIR SUPPLY
YEADON
THE NORTH'S LEADING AVIATION STORE

Airband Radios, Scanners, Magazines, Timetables, Books, Prints, Film, Photoprocessing, Models and Pilot's Flying clothing and Supplies

97 HIGH STREET, YEADON, LEEDS, LS19 7TA

Just around the corner from Leeds Bradford Airport

OPENING HOURS 10 AM TO 5 PM
TUESDAY TO SATURDAY, CLOSED
SUNDAY AND MONDAY

Mail Order Catalogue: £1.50 refundable
or Phone: Ken Cothliff on 0113 250 9581
Fax: 0113 250 0119

Contents

Abbreviations	3
Introduction	5
AB Airlines/Air Bristol	8
Air 2000	9
Air Atlantique	11
Air Foyle	11
Air Kilroe	12
Air South West	12
Airtours International Airways	13
Air UK	15
Airworld	15
Atlantic Airlines	16
Aurigny Air Services	19
BAC Express Airlines	20
Britannia Airways	21
British Airways	25
British International Helicopters	31
British Mediterranean Airways	31
British Midland Airways	32
British Regional Airlines	36
British World Airlines	38
Brymon Airways	41
Business Air	43
Caledonian Airways	45
Channel Express	47
CityFlyer Express	49
Classic Airways	50
Debonair Airways	51
easyJet Airline	53
Emerald Airways	54
European Airways	56
European Aviation Air Charter	56
Euroscot Express	60
Flightline	61
Flying Colours Airlines	63
GB Airways	63
Gill Airways	64
Go	65
HeavyLift Cargo Airlines	66
Hunting Cargo Airlines	68
Isles of Scilly Skybus	69
Jersey European Airways	69
KLM uk	72
Leisure International Airways	74
Loganair	76
Love Air	77
Maersk Air Ltd	77
Manx Airlines	78
Monarch Airlines	81
Peach Air	83
Sabre Airways	83
Sky-Trek Airlines	84
South Coast Airways	84
Streamline Aviation	85
Suckling Airways	85
Titan Airways	88
TNT International	89
Virgin Atlantic Airways	93

Abbreviations

AOC	Air Operator's Certificate	CAA	Civil Aviation Authority
BA	British Airways	IT	Inclusive Tour
BAC	British Aircraft Corporation	KLM	Royal Dutch Airlines
BEA	British European Airways	SAS	Scandinavian Airlines System
BOAC	British Overseas Airways Corporation		

NOW YOU HAVE PURCHASED ABC UK AIRLINES WHY NOT EXPAND YOUR KNOWLEDGE WITH THE 'TAHS' RANGE OF SPECIALIST BOOKS FOR THE ENTHUSIAST, HISTORIAN OR SPOTTER?

AIRBAND RADIOS
We stock a range of top quality airband radios, with prices starting at £139.00. Details of all the radios stocked are included in our catalogue 1.

AIRLINES '98
The 16th edition available now is the established favourite for coverage of the world's airline fleet listingS. Every airline in the world where aircraft from light twin to wide bodies are operated. 170 countries, 1,700 airlines, over 25,000 registrations. Each aircraft is listed with registration, type, c/n, p/i, and where applicable line and fleet number and name. Available as Comb Bound (ie metal lay flat binding) at just £8.95 or in a loose leaf binder at £12.95.

AIRPORT MOVEMENTS
is a monthly magazine published and distributed by THE AVIATION HOBBY SHOP, AIRPORT MOVEMENTS gives airport movements on a regular basis from the following airports: Heathrow, Gatwick, Stansted, Luton, Birmingham, Shannon, Bournemouth, Bristol, Cardiff, East Midlands, Jersey, Northolt, Southampton, Southend as well as foreign airport reports on a space available basis. Average monthly page content is around 28. AIRPORT MOVEMENTS is available around the 15th to the 20th of the month from a number of different outlets in the South of England, the Midlands and the Manchester area at a price of 75p per copy. However, should you wish to have a regular standing order for this publication to be dispatched hot from the press we will be more than happy to place your name on our regular mailing list. To have your own copy of AIRPORT MOVEMENTS sent to you each month costs £1 per copy and this includes first-class mail delivery in the UK. You can subscribe for three, six or 12 months. To receive a free sample copy of our choice send a stamped 9in x 6in envelope.

PISTON ENGINED AIRLINER PRODUCTION LIST
The second edition of the Piston Engined Airliner Production List was published in December 1996. Fully revised and updated production and service histories of EVERY MAJOR WESTERN - BUILT PISTON ENGINED AIRLINER to enter service since World War II. Each aircraft is listed by manufacturer and type in construction number sequence. Each individual entry then lists line number (if applicable), sub-type, and first flight date if known. The entry then goes on to list every known registration carried by the airframe, owners and delivery of purchase date, lease dates, crash or withdrawn from service dates, and any other relevant information regarding the airframe. The comprehensive list of aircraft types covered includes:- Airspeed Ambassador, ATL 98 Carvair, Avro Tudor, Avro York, BN.2A Mk.III Trislander, Boeing 377 Statocruiser, Bristol 170 Freighter/Wayfarer, Canadair North Star/Argonaut, Convair 240, Convair 340/440, Curtiss C-46 Commando, deHavilland DH.114 Heron, DouglasC-54/DC-4 Skymaster, Douglas DC-6, Douglas DC-7, Handley Page Halifax 8/Halton, Handley Page Hermes, Lockheed l-049 Constellation, Lockheed L-649/647 Constellation, Lockheed L-1049 Super Constellation, Lockheed L-1649 Starliner, Martin 2-0-2/4-0-4, Miles/Handley Page Marathon, SAAB Scandia, Scottish Aviation Twin Pioneer, Vickers Viking.

The source information used is based on the comprehensive data base of Lundkvist Aviation Research (publishers of Aviation Letter) and is used with their co-operation and assistance. LAR/Aviation Letter are world renowned as leaders in the field of airliner information and can be reliied upon for the topical and accurate data. Other information has been gleaned from many other sources and added to the data base making this the most comprehensive production list ever to be published on pison engined airliners. PISTON ENGINED AIRLINER PRODUCTION LIST contains just under 500 pages and is available in a handy A5 size and available in four formats:- (1) Soft-back in card covers with comb binding price **£13.95**; (2) Refill pages for those already have a loose-leaf binder price **£13.95**; (3) Square bound - with heavy duty metal stitching at price **£13.95**; (4) or in a loose-leaf binder at price **£17.95**.

WORLD AIRLINE FLEET NEWS
Published monthly, World Airline Fleet News is dedicated to the ever changing and exciting world of airlines and airliners-reporting new airlines, new and used airliner transactions, livery changes and much more. Unrivalled photographic coverage on a worldwide basis is complimented by the generous use of colour. Each issue contains approximately 50 illustrations with around 30 in colour. World Airline Fleet News is produced on quality gloss art paper for the best photographic reproduction. Sample issue **£3.25**.

JET AIRLINER PRODUCTION LIST Volume 1 - BOEING
Published in September 1997, Jet Airliner Production List - Volume 1 - BOEING has been completely revised and updated. Jet Airliner Production List gives full production and service histories of EVERY BOEING - BUILT JET AIRLINER that has entered service since the start of the Jet age. Each aircraft is listed by manufacturer and type in construction number sequence. Each individual entry then lists line number (where applicable), sub-type, and first flight date where known. The entry then goes on to list every registration carried by the airframe, owners and delivery dates, leases crash or withdrawal from service dates and any other relevant information. There is a complete cross reference of registration to c/n for every type covered. TYPES COVERED INCLUDE:- BOEING 707/720; **BOEING 727; BOEING 737; BOEING 737 new generation; BOEING 747; BOEING 757; BOEING 767; BOEING 777**. Jet Airliner Production List - Volume 1 - BOEING is available in a handy A5 size and is available in a choice of finish [1] comb bound lay-flat price **£10.95**; [2] Square bound with metal stitching and wrap around cover price **£10.95**; [3] Refill pages for those already have a loose-leaf binder price **£10.95**; [4] Loose-leaf Binder edition price **£14.95**.

WORLD AIRLINE FLEETS DIRECTORY 1998
The second edition of this joint Aviation Hobby Shop/Aviation Data Center title was published in January 1998. Completely updated to press time with all the latest changes and new information. Large A4 format with easy to read text.197 countries; Over 3,000 airlines, operators & water tanker fleets; Over 33,000 registrations; Over 400 pages; Over 4,000 changes & amendments since last edition; Current to 15th December. World Airline Fleets Directory 1998 is available in a handy A4 size and is available in a choice of finish. [1] comb bound lay-flat price **£16.95**; [2] Square bound with metal stitching price **£16.95**; [3] Refill pages for those already have a loose-leaf binder price **£16.95**; [4] Loose-leaf Binder edition price **£19.95**. AVAILABLE NOW

TURBOPROP AIRLINER PRODUCTION LIST
To be Published in spring 1998, the third edition of Turbo Prop Airliner Production List gives full production and service histories of EVERY WESTERN - BUILT TURBOPROP AIRLINER
to enter service since 1948. Each aircraft is listed by manufacturer and type in construction number sequence. Each individual entry then lists line number (where applicable), sub-type, and first flight date where known. The entry then goes on to list every registration carried by the airframe, owners and delivery dates, leases, crash or withdrawal from service dates and any other relevant information. There is a complete cross reference of registration to c/n for every type covered. Over 400 pages. **TYPES COVERED INCLUDE** :- AEROSPATIALE/AERITALIA ATR 42/72, Armstrong-Whitworth Argosy, Avro (BAe) 748, Beech 99; Beech 1900, British Aerospace ATP, British Aerospace Jetstream 31, British Aerospace Jetstream 41, Bristol Britania; Canadair CL-44, CASA/Nurtanio 212, CASA/Nurtanio 235, Convair 580; Convair 600, Convair 640 dehavilland DHC-6 Twin Otter, dehavilland DHC-7; dehavilland DHC-8, Dornier/HAL 228; Dornier 328, Embraer Emb.110 Bandeirante, Embraer Emb.120 Brasilia, Fairchild/Swearingen Merlin/Metro, Fairchild F-27; Fairchild FH-227, Fokker F.27; Fokker 50; GAF Nomad; Frumman G.159 Gulfstream, Handley Page HPR.7 Herald, Handley Page HP.137 Jetstream, HAL748; IAI Arava, Lockheed 100 Hercules, Lockheed 188 Electra, NAMC YS-11; Nord 262, SAAB 340; SAAB 2000, Saunders ST-27; Shorts SC-7 Skyvan, Shorts 330; Shorts 360, Vickers Vanguard; Vickers Viscount. Turbo Prop Airliner Productions List - is available in a handy A5 size and is available in a choice of finish [1] comb bound lay-flat price **£11.95**; [2] Square bound with metal stitching and around cover price **£11.95**; [3] Refill pages for those already have a loose-leaf binder price **£11.95**; [4] Loose-leaf Binder edition price **£15.95**.

GREAT AIRLINERS - BOEING 747SP
Number three in the Great Airliners series, the Boeing 747SP. Though produced in small numbers the short-body version of Boeing's legendary jumbo has enjoyed enormous operational success, filling in on long-haul thin traffic routes. The author presents this fascinating story with extensive coverage of the SP's concept, development and airline operations, along with individual histories and photos of each aircraft built. **£16.95**

GREAT AIRLINERS - THE DOUGLAS DC-8
Terry Waddington covers the first turbine example to evolve from the famous DC Series of airliners built by Douglas. The DC-8 story includes earlier designs by the same name which never came to fruition, and reviews events leading to the Eight as we know today. Exceptional colour photography - much of it air-to-air - provides the reader with a visual record of the airplanes heritage. From its basic model to several stretched versions and the re-engined examples that continue to operate today, the author, who had insider's view, provides a definite history of the DC-8. **£16.95**

GREAT AIRLINERS - CONVAIR 880/990
Jon Proctor tells the facinating story of Convair's attempt to corner the early medium-range jetliner market with the 880, followed by the 990, a combined program that nearly bankrupted a major corporation. Individual histories and photos of all 102 aircraft are provided (a unique feature in any book!) and include every colour scheme ever worn by a Convair jet. Production and flight testing is reviewed, plus airline service by major 880 and 990 operators. Separate chapters address military applications and accidents. **£16.95**

AIRLINES TO EUROPE 1998
Following the excellement response to the first two editions of Airlines to Europe, the 1997 edition is now available. As with the first two editions we have taken the main data base and stripped out any airlines or aircraft not likely to be seen in Europe. Airlines to Europe only lists (1) aircraft registration, (2) Aircraft type and (3) constructors number and line number if applicable. Colour cover and one hundred pages. **£3.99**

FREE CATALOGUES
All our goods are listed in our two free catalogues. Catalogue 1 books, colour prints and airband radios. Catalogue 2: plastic kits, decals and modelling accessories. Write, ring or fax for your free copy today.

We are just 10 minutes drive from Heathrow Airport, just off the M4/M25 motorways. Bus U3 operates between Heathrow Central and West Drayton BR station, two minutes walk from the shop. All major credit cards accepted. 24hr 'Ansaphone' service.

The Aviation Hobby Shop

(Dept ABC), 4 HORTON PARADE, HORTON ROAD, WEST DRAYTON, MIDDLESEX UB7 8EA
Tel: 01895 442123   Fax: 01895 421412

Introduction

Since taking the first cautious steps soon after the end of World War 1, the airline industry has been developed to the point when nowadays it is taken very much for granted by business and leisure travellers alike. In the pioneering 1920s there were few from either category using this form of transport which competed with the more traditional and reliable trains. In inclement weather the latter were faster and certainly safer than aircraft, especially since headwinds often forced a refuelling stop to be made along the route. A lack of suitable airfields near to the destination did not help and of course there were no navigation aids. It was common practice for pilots to follow railway lines from station to station, which in many cases had their names painted on the roof of the buildings to give pilots a clue to their whereabouts. Most of the equipment employed for both domestic and international flights was ex-military, there being a glut of surplus stock no longer needed for more belligerent purposes. In their converted form the ex-bombers carried a dozen or so passengers together with a token amount of freight usually comprised of newspapers.

Some progress was made during the 1920s, especially in 1924 when the merger of several independents created Imperial Airways, which then became the British national carrier. However, the company's main interest concerned the opening of links with the far-flung areas of the empire or the fashionable holiday locations in France and Switzerland.

The hitherto neglected domestic market received some attention towards the end of the decade when an experimental service was introduced by Imperial to link London, Birmingham, Manchester and Liverpool. It was one of the few domestic operations available and carried some 600 passengers in its three months' period of operation.

Development of such services was therefore left to small airlines that often owed their existence to bus companies. The 1930s produced many such examples, the first being Hillman Airways, a well-known north London coach operator of the day. It was an early attempt to offer a low-cost, no-frills operation with fares set at a level that were within the reach of many more people. It was a concept that had been applied to the company's coach business and it proved equally successful with the air services. It also prompted the launch of a steady stream of new airlines, including Railway Air Services, a carrier somewhat reluctantly formed by the railways in response to the growing popularity of air travel. It tended to concentrate its activities on the trunk routes, leaving the shorter and more seasonal sectors to the smaller independents.

The postal authorities also noted the benefits of air transport and duly awarded contracts for the movement of mail. Initially lifting some 500lb (226.8kg) daily, by the outbreak of World War 2 in 1939 an annual total of about 450,000lb (204,120kg) was being carried by the airlines involved.

The next five years or so proved the value of air travel for both freight and passengers, but when peace was restored in 1945 a similar situation existed to that of 25 years earlier. Once again a considerable number of aircraft suddenly became surplus to requirements, which encouraged the creation of small airlines by ex-RAF pilots with the vivid memory of flying still fresh. Full of optimism, much of their demob money was invested in a single aircraft to fulfil the dream of commercial operations, yet sadly few survived for very long in the difficult times when government policy did not favour the independents. Instead, British European Airways took over the services previously handled by companies such as Railway Air Services, assuming the responsibility for both domestic and continental operations.

It was a bleak period for the independents, but unintentionally the Russians provided help in 1948 with the blockade of Berlin. The resulting airlift was not only the salvation of the German city, but the work proved a lifeline for the participating carriers. Those involved had their fleets of converted bombers operating alongside the military types for the duration of the emergency. While bringing a welcome injection of funds, for many it was only a temporary respite. There was little work available for the larger types when the blockade was lifted in 1949, quickly bringing the end of more companies.

Nevertheless it was apparent that the national carrier was unable to cope unaided, so applications were invited for licences to fly on some of the seasonal routes, usually those with little hope of a profitable future. While this opportunity was of no consolation to most of the ex-airlift carriers, one of the exceptions was the independent operator Aquila Airways, which proposed to use its converted Sunderland flying boats to link the south coast with Scotland. There were no apparent problems for the scheme and indeed a proving flight confirmed the feasibility of the venture. Unluckily, advance bookings were so poor that the airline was forced to abandon the idea before any revenue-earning sorties were carried out. Cornwall was still very much in the future for Scottish holidaymakers, who still favoured Dunoon or Rothesay for their annual excursions.

The slow growth of the small independents was really the key factor in their ability to remain in business. The fleets usually contained cheap ex-RAF aircraft, such as Dominies, which on conversion became Rapides. This reliable type was readily available and was acceptable to the travelling public, but inevitably the ageing machines eventually had to be replaced in the name of progress. By the mid-1950s carriers were therefore forced into the bigger and more expensive leagues, which all too often heralded their demise. This unsatisfactory state of affairs continued for some years until competition was allowed on some of the main trunk routes in the UK. British Eagle in particular made impressive advances in the early 1960s by introducing modern types on to the London/Scottish services, forcing BEA to respond. The company also played a significant role in the development of the Inclusive Tours (ITs) when it used Britannias to carry holidaymakers to the Mediterranean resorts at amazingly low fares.

Gradually independents were given more freedom to operate scheduled services, although they still had to receive the approval of the appropriate authority. Despite the growth in air travel, generally the flights offered were single sector operations since there was apparently little demand for a multi-stop trip. It therefore came as a surprise when such a scheme was announced by Channel Airways, one of the few surviving carriers from the immediate postwar period and one that produced more original ideas than the majority of its contemporaries. Convinced that there was a demand, Channel proposed to employ a jet for the trunk element and a smaller turboprop type as a feeder. The route envisaged linked Stansted with Aberdeen, with a BAC One-Eleven making a number of short stops at airports *en route*. Feeder connections were made at a number of points with either an HS748 or Heron, but when the so-called Scottish Flyer eventually started in January 1969, a Viscount had replaced the jet for economic reasons.

It was not really surprising that the service soon began to run into trouble. Crew scheduling was not at all simple when so many landings were involved, with sectors averaging only 65 miles. Handling staff were needed at intermediate points, while load factors fluctuated enormously; the trunk centre sections received good support but the ends were very poorly patronised. It was a novel idea but before its time, since the British public was not ready to visit the supermarket by air. Ironically, within a year the North Sea oil and gas projects were responsible for a vast increase in traffic at Aberdeen, but it was too late for Channel since the airline had suspended the service after 10 months due to the continuing losses. Within three years Channel itself had disappeared into history, another example of an airline which failed to survive the transition into the jet age, this time through over-ambition. During the following 25 years the pattern remained much the same with the loss of various small carriers overshadowed by the departure of Air Europe, British Caledonian and Dan-Air.

The present day UK airline industry is the result of numerous takeovers and mergers, involving both large and small companies. In 1993 there was a new development when British Airways announced its intention to offer franchise agreements to selected carriers. As a result, some of the familiar names and liveries disappeared from the aircraft, to be replaced with that of the flag carrier. While it is sad that the airlines' visual identity has been lost, the companies included in the arrangement have reported increased business. Low-cost operations have also been introduced, easyJet becoming the first to offer such services in 1995, followed in June 1996 by Debonair, both carriers being based at Luton. Their growing popularity did not go unnoticed by British Airways, so after a lengthy period of evaluation it announced that a low-cost subsidiary was being launched in the spring of 1998 to compete in this market.

Several airlines such as European Aviation and British World have recognised the need for back-up aircraft to cover technical delays or provide additional capacity at short notice. As a result, both airlines' fleet members are kept busy fulfilling these requirements on short- or long-term leases. A number of plants around the world have been engaged in the conversion of Airbus A300s and A310s into freighters, the first examples in the UK entering service with both Channel Express and HeavyLift in the autumn of 1997. The overnight movement of all types of freight continues to be carried by TNT which has been collecting more Boeing 727s to add to its BAe 146 fleet. Although ideal for the carrier's needs, unless the trijet can be hush-kitted to meet the 2002 Stage 3 noise regulations, the type will have to be replaced within three years or so.

Over-ambition and an apparent lack of research have been responsible for many failures in the past 50 years and doubtless there will be more. Replacement carriers will be forthcoming, yet in some cases it will be difficult to understand the logic in their choice of routes when nothing seems to indicate that success is possible. At least all the airlines covered in this book are current, but then no airline official is going to admit to an imminent demise!

UK Passenger Figures 1996

Air 2000	4,750,000
Airtours International	4,589,000
Air UK	3,626,000
Britannia Airways	7,540,000
British Airways	33,170,000
British Midland	5,320,000
Caledonian Airways	2,292,400
CityFlyer Express	932,000
Debonair	600,000
Jersey European Airways	1,545,000
Manx Airlines/British Regional	1,556,100
Monarch Airlines	4,550,000
Virgin Atlantic Airways	2,292,400

Above:
RA-82044 — Antonov An-124 of HeavyLift/VolgaDnepr.

AB Airlines/Air Bristol
(7L/AZX)
Head Office: Enterprise House, Stansted Airport, Essex CM24 1QW
Tel: (01279) 680909   Fax: (01279) 680443

When Air Bristol was formed in 1993 it was with the intention of providing a scheduled service network radiating from Bristol/Filton, an airfield located nearer to the city than Lulsgate. Although having the support of the owner, British Aerospace, the scheme did not meet the approval of the local council.

Planning consent was therefore delayed and a subsequent public inquiry ruled against the project. In the meantime Air Bristol continued its charter operations which included the daily link between Filton and Toulouse on behalf of British Aerospace Airbus. This is operated with a One-Eleven leased from Bournemouth-based European Aviation with the aircraft configured in a business class interior.

In March 1995 the Group launched Air Belfast which began frequent services between Stansted and Belfast International on 1 March using a pair of leased One-Elevens. There was every expectation that the recently agreed peace plan for Northern Ireland would encourage an influx of visitors, but while loads on the service were generally as forecast, on 21 March 1996 the airline dropped the route. This was partly due to further instances of unrest in the province which dampened any likelihood of any rapid improvement in load factors, but also because of the arrival of a competitor: Jersey European already operated to Belfast City with a 146, but had decided to expand its coverage by adding International as an alternative.

By this time the Air Bristol Group had already started another project by launching AB Shannon to operate a twice-daily scheduled service between Gatwick and Shannon. Starting on 7 December 1995, it has since proved a very successful venture with a frequency increase necessary to three times daily during the summer season in 1996. This period brought the airline load factors of some 80% and well within reach of its target of 100,000 passengers in the first year.

A second route was started by the airline on 1 May 1997, this time linking Gatwick and Lisbon on a daily basis with a One-Eleven configured with a two-class cabin. In the meantime the company had changed its name to AB Airlines thereby simplifying the One-Elevens' livery, which was that of European Aviation but with AB titles and logo. The airline expects Expo 98 at the Portuguese capital to attract many visitors and a corresponding increase in traffic during the summer. This will be carried by one of the two Boeing 737-300s that AB plans to introduce in May together with an increase in frequency to two trips per day on the route.

Some quickly prepared expansion came on 1 December 1997 when the airline became the first to operate a scheduled service between Gatwick and Berlin Schönefeld. The decision was taken after the surprise withdrawal of Deutsche BA and Lufthansa, although AB had already been evaluating the route. In the early days the timings tended to favour German-originating traffic, but this was due to change in the spring of 1998 when a twice-daily rotation with a 737-300 was planned. However, it is by no means certain that the One-Elevens will be returned to the lessor since they may prove useful to build up new routes during the early stages.

AB has a number of possible destinations under evaluation, including a Stansted-Shannon and Birmingham-Shannon service, due to be launched on 22 May probably using the same aircraft to fly both sectors. With the introduction of its two 737-300s, the airline will be reverting to its own house colours of purple and green which have not been seen since the Air Belfast days. In the longer term, deposits have already been placed on six of the new generation 737-700s with deliveries starting in 2001.

FLEET:

Regn	Series	C/n
BAC One-Eleven		
G-AVMI	510ED	137
G-AVMN	510ED	142
G-AVMW	510ED	150

Regn	Series	C/n
Boeing 737		
G-OABA	300	-
G-	300	-
-		

Above:
G-AVMW — BAC One-Eleven 510ED of AB Airlines. *AST Photography*

Below:
G-OOOJ — Boeing 757-23A of Air 2000.

Air 2000 (DP/AMM)
Head Office: First Choice House, London Road, Crawley, West Sussex RH10 2GX
Tel: (01293) 518966   Fax: (01293) 588757

The Manchester-based airline was formed in 1986, with operations commencing on 11 April 1987 when a Boeing 757 registered G-OOOA flew a load of IT passengers to Malaga.

Above:
G-OOAB — Airbus A320-231 of Air 2000.

Although not a particularly unusual event, it marked the start of a significant change in the standard of service offered by the charter industry generally.

Created by the former managing director of Air Europe, Errol Cossey, the name Air 2000 was chosen for the subsidiary of the Owners Abroad Group, a major British tour operator. After the evaluation of suitable equipment the Boeing 757-200 was chosen, whereupon arrangements were made to lease an initial two examples of the type. In preparation for the launch, the recruitment of flightdeck crews resulted in 26 pilots with more than 200,000hr between them attending a conversion course at the Boeing Training Center in Seattle.

Before the end of April the airline had two aircraft on strength, enabling the carrier to undertake 35 sorties per week to 12 of the popular Mediterranean destinations during the summer season. Almost immediately Air 2000 established a reputation for its outstanding quality of service, which quickly began to cause concern amongst competitors. The initiative in offering new in-flight video entertainment, attractively presented hot meals, complimentary champagne, newspapers, sweets and hot cotton towels was appreciated by the travelling public. It became the expected standard which others were forced to emulate if they were to remain in business.

By 1990 Air 2000's fleet had grown to eight B757s plus a single 148-seat Boeing 737-300 which was operated from the beginning of 1989 until the end of the 1990 summer season. At this stage the airline was flying an intensive series of IT services from Manchester and Glasgow both to European and US destinations, becoming the first carrier to operate direct flights between the Scottish airport and Orlando, Florida. This followed a successful challenge to the government's Prestwick policies in the courts, backed by considerable support from would-be transatlantic travellers. During the year Gatwick was added to the airline's departure points, providing seats for tour operators other than its Owners Abroad parent. It also achieved the distinction of being ranked fourth in a survey on leisure airlines conducted by *Holiday Which* — the only UK carrier to appear amongst the top five.

Other long-haul routes were duly added to the network, including Kenya, Mexico and the Caribbean area, while an application to the CAA resulted in the award of a scheduled licence to serve Larnaca and Paphos, Cyprus. The island was linked with Gatwick when the operation began in October 1993, although the service was subsequently extended to Birmingham and Manchester. However, Air 2000 did not intend to expand any further into this market, preferring to remain a leading charter carrier.

Meanwhile, the number of airports served by the airline steadily increased with bases at Birmingham, Bristol, Dublin, Gatwick, Glasgow, Manchester and Newcastle. There was also a presence at East Midlands, Exeter, Luton and Stansted but on a smaller scale, often using the four 179-seat Airbus A320s that joined the fleet in 1992. A change of parent resulted from the takeover of Owners Abroad by First Choice Holidays which led to the addition of this name on the forward fuselage of Air 2000's aircraft. Some 70% of the latter's flying is carried out on behalf of the parent company, but more than 120 other companies also use the popular carrier to transport clients.

One of the secrets of Air 2000's success over the past years has been its willingness to listen to its customers' comments and the introduction of innovative practices ahead of competitors. This constant improvement of the product has helped to maintain its lead, the latest development being the new livery applied in the spring of 1997, although whether it is noted and appreciated by the average passenger is debatable. Future expansion will involve the addition of a Boeing 767-300ER in April 1999 for use on the long-haul routes, with a second due to arrive one year later.

FLEET:

Regn	Series	C/n
Airbus A320		
G-OOAA	231	291
G-OOAB	231	292
G-OOAC	231	327
G-OOAD	231	336
Boeing 757		
G-OOOA	28A	23767
G-OOOB	28A	23822
G-OOOC	28A	24017
G-OOOD	28A	24235
G-OOOG	23A	24292
G-OOOI	23A	24289
G-OOOJ	23A	24290
G-OOOS	236	24397
G-OOOU	2Y0	25240
G-OOOV	225	22211
G-OOOW	225	22611
G-OOOX	2Y0	26158
G-	2Q8	28203
Boeing 767		
G-	300ER	-
G-	300ER	-

Air Atlantique (AAG)

See Atlantic Airlines

Air Foyle (GS/UPA)

Head Office: Halcyon House, London Luton International Airport, Luton, Bedfordshire LU2 9LU

Tel: (01582) 419792　　Fax: (01582) 400958

When Air Foyle was founded in May 1978 its operations mainly involved air taxi activities from Luton. Through the years the company has been divided into two sections with Air Foyle Ltd (AFL) being responsible for the cargo services and Air Foyle Charter Ltd (AFCAL) handling the passenger operations. The latter was created in 1994 specifically to operate the larger commercial aircraft, a task it has subsequently performed for Airworld, easyJet Airline, Sabre Airways, the Sunseekers Leisure Group and Virgin Express. Another customer signed a five-year contract with Air Foyle in November 1997 which will entail the operation of a pair of ex-Finnair A300s for the UK newcomer Air Scandic from 1998.

Air Foyle Ltd is involved in two distinct types of cargo operations. Since May 1987 a number of BAe 146s have been operated on behalf of TNT, with schedules that take the aircraft to numerous European airports, usually flying four sectors of about 1hr each per night. At other times, such as during the day and at weekends, the aircraft are available for charter which includes the movement of racehorses and other livestock needing rapid transportation in relative comfort.

Following the breakup of the Soviet Union, there have been several partnerships established, one being that between Air Foyle and the Antonov Design Bureau. As a result, the two companies have had an agreement since 1989 concerning the worldwide operation of the An-124 Ruslan and IL-76 freighters. During these occasions, the UK carrier has achieved over 10,000hr of airborne time and has carried over 46,000 tonnes of outsized cargo, plus some 7,000 tonnes of supplies destined for relief organisations around the world.

Aircrews for both types are supplied by the Ukrainian airline, with maintenance normally performed at Kiev.

FLEET:

Regn	Series	C/n
Antonov An-124		
UR-82007	100	19530501005
UR-82008	100	19530501006
UR-82009	100	19530501007
UR-82027	100	19539502288
UR-82029	100	19530502630
BAe 146 See under TNT		
Ilyushin IL-76		
UR-78755	-	0083484531

Air Kilroe (9R/AKL)

Head Office: A Pier, Terminal 1, Manchester International Airport, Manchester M90 3PF
Tel: (0161) 436 2055   Fax: (0161) 499 1890

Manchester has been the airline's operating base since it was formed in 1978 to provide an air taxi service. The company diversified in September 1993 with the introduction of a scheduled service between Manchester and Cardiff using a Jetstream 31, but this was later discontinued. Regular links are maintained between the northwest airport and Teesside on behalf of ICI, while contract charters are also flown for the Ministry of Defence.

FLEET:

Regn	Series	C/n
BAe Jetstream 31		
G-IJYS	3102	715
G-OAKA	3102	640
G-OAKI	3102	718
G-OAKJ	3202	795

Air South West (8H/PIE)

Head Office: Plymouth City Airport, Roborough, Plymouth, Devon PL6 8BW
Tel: (01752) 770055   Fax: (01752) 770097

When formed in May 1993 the company took the name of Newquay Air since its operations involved schedules from the West Country airport. It was not long before the airline moved its base to Exeter, coinciding with a name change to Air South West, although it generally continued with the same route network. Subsequently its head office was moved to Plymouth from where the carrier began regular flights to Cork, Dublin and Manchester. However, these were later suspended, leaving the daily link between Cork and Belfast as the only service in March 1998. Other routes are expected to be introduced.

FLEET:

Regn	Series	C/n
Embraer EMB-110 Bandeirante		
G-AGYT	P1	234
PA-31 Navajo Chieftain		
G-GRAM	350	31-7305006

Airtours International Airways (VZ/AIH)

Head Office: Parkway Three, Parkway Business Centre, 300 Princess Road, Manchester M14 7QU
Tel: (0161) 232 6600   Fax: (0161) 232 6610

There has been considerable growth in the Airtours Group since the company began trading as a small Burnley-based agency in the 1970s. In the early days it contracted its flying requirements to various airlines operating mainly from Manchester, the largest share being handled by Dan-Air which was entrusted with 65% of the clients.

While generally satisfied with the arrangements, in early 1990 there were signs that it would be prudent to reduce this dependence by taking over the air travel element of the short-haul packages. By the time that the Board had met in May to review the strategy for the company's five-year plan, the industry had lost Novair, Paramount and British Island from the charter market. There was therefore a real danger that Airtours would be subject to higher costs and uncertainties, yet still be without protection from any future failures.

The situation was reviewed with some urgency, resulting in the go-ahead for the scheme to create an in-house airline known as Airtours International. All of the available aircraft types were carefully evaluated until the MD-83 was finally chosen, largely because of passenger preference for five-abreast seating rather than the more common 3+3 layout. The traffic figures indicated that a fleet of five aircraft would be sufficient to cover 90% of the programme, the remaining 10% being carried by Monarch, Air 2000 and Caledonian on long-haul services.

The fledgling airline was therefore ready to operate its first service between its Manchester base and Rhodes on 20 March 1991, a trip repeated later in the day from Birmingham. The airline also intended to out-station an MD-83 at Stansted for the summer, but it was by chance that a non-revenue-earning charter became one of the first movements at the much-acclaimed terminal's opening day. The impressive growth rate of the Group continued with more MD-83s joining the fleet, which was further increased in size in 1993 when Airtours took over Cardiff-based Aspro Holidays in November 1993. This also included the latter's associated carrier Inter European, which brought with it a pair of Airbus A320s and two Boeing 757s. Airtours had previously added two 767s to its

Above:
G-CSVS — Boeing 757-236 of Airtours International Airways.

collection so that it could undertake its own long-haul charter flights to the US and Caribbean, destinations that were growing in popularity.

After operating the two Airbus machines for some time, the carrier decided to standardise on this type at the expense of the MD-83s which had been the backbone of the fleet. A number of secondhand A320s were obtained from various sources so that by the 1996 summer season the type was flying all of the carrier's European sorties. Meanwhile, Airtours had acquired Spies, a Scandinavian leisure group, together with its large charter airline Premiair. The latter also operated the A320, so it enabled Airtours to standardise its own fleet by transferring aircraft on a one-for-one basis between the two carriers. A common livery was also adopted to complete the exchange process in time for the 1997 season.

Nowadays Airtours has departure points at Belfast, Birmingham, Bristol, Cardiff, East Midlands, Gatwick, Glasgow, Humberside, Leeds/Bradford, Liverpool, Manchester, Newcastle, Stansted and Teesside. A wide range of long-haul services are now offered across the Atlantic, with destinations in Africa and Australia also experiencing growth. The latter route will be operated by Airbus A330s from April and June 1999, two specimens having been ordered to replace the 767s.

Fleet:

Regn	Series	C/n
Airbus A320		
G-COEZ	231	179
G-CRPH	231	424
G-DAJR	231	164
G-EPFR	231	437
G-RDVE	231	163
G-SUEE	231	363
G-TICL	231	169
G-TMDP	231	168
G-TPTT	212	348
G-VCED	231	193
G-YJBM	231	362
Airbus A330		
G-	200	-
G-	200	-
Boeing 757		
G-CSVS	236	25620
G-JALC	225	22194
G-LCRC	23A	24636
G-MCEA	225	22200
G-PIDS	225	22195
G-RJGR	225	22197
G-WJAN	21K	28674
Boeing 767		
G-DAJC	31KER	27206
G-DIMB	31KER	28865
G-SJMC	31KER	27205

Above:
G-TPTT — Airbus A320-212 of Airtours International.

Air UK (UK/UKA)
See KLM uk

Above:
G-UKFC — Fokker 100 of Air UK. To become KLM uk.

Airworld (RL/AWD)
Head Office: 25 Elmfield Road, Bromley, Kent BR1 1LT
Tel: (0181) 325 3200   Fax: (0181) 325 3209

In the early 1990s the UK tour operator Iberotravel employed Inter European Airways for its clients' travel arrangements, but with the takeover of the latter by Airtours, the

Above:
G-BXAW — Airbus A321-211 of Airworld Aviation.

company decided to form its own airline.
Known as Airworld, the carrier was formed in October 1993 with operations commencing in the following April from Bristol, Cardiff and Manchester with two Airbus A320s. At the end of the first season activities were suspended for the winter, restarting in the spring of 1995 with the delivery of a third A320. The fleet was further expanded in April 1997 when Airworld became the first UK airline to take delivery of an Airbus A321, a second specimen following a year later. In the meantime, four new A320s had replaced the original trio which were returned to the lessor. Now 100% owned by Sunworld, itself a part of the Thomas Cook Group, the airline continues to fly IT charters not only for its parent, but also for more than 30 other tour operators. While operations from Bristol, Cardiff and Manchester have successfully continued, the airline also has a busy programme at Gatwick and Glasgow. Equipment is also leased to other carriers in off-peak periods.

FLEET:

Regn	Series	C/n
Airbus A320		
G-BXKA	214	714
G-BXKB	214	716
G-BXKC	214	730
G-BXKD	214	735
G-BXRW	231	308
G-BXRX	231	314
Airbus A321		
G-BXAW	211	666
G-BXNP	211	775

Atlantic Airlines (AAG)

Head Office: Hangar 5, Coventry Airport, Baginton, Coventry CV8 3AZ
Tel: (01203) 307566   Fax: (01203) 639037

The Air Atlantique Group consists of a number of companies, the latest being Atlantic Airlines which was created in early 1998 to cover the passenger and cargo operations of the organisation. Its career started as a Jersey-based air-taxi operator known as General Aviation Services in 1969, but in 1977 there was a change of name when the company began charter work with a DC-3. It was not long before more of the venerable machines were added to the fleet, which took up residence at Coventry. During the mid-1980s the airline also operated from a base at Stansted where the company's Bristol Freighter was a familiar sight. However, since the airport was earmarked for development and the premises occupied were due to disappear under acres of concrete, Air Atlantique wisely returned to Coventry.

Subsequently, the DC-3 fleet has been involved in patrol work connected with oil spillages around the British coastline, for which sideways-looking radar, infra-red detection and ultra-violet sensor equipment is carried by the aircraft. While the majority of the DC-3s are involved in such duties or are stored, two are employed for the airline's contract freight movements alongside a pair of DC-6s and five Lockheed Electras, the first of which was introduced in 1995.

The airline has been involved in scheduled passenger services on at least two occasions, starting in 1988 when an elderly Avro 748 was leased from Euroair to undertake services between Southampton and the Channel Islands. In order to keep fares at a low level, a direct-sell method was adopted for reservations, thereby avoiding the commission normally payable to travel agents for their so-called expertise. Unfortunately, it took time to convert travellers to this procedure which resulted in slow growth for the airline. This forced an early suspension of the venture at the end of the first summer season, when the 748 was returned to the lessor.

In 1992 a Fairchild Metro was leased by Air Atlantique for scheduled service use by its subsidiary, Air Corbière, although in practice a Cessna F406 Caravan was usually substituted. This time the Channel Islands were linked with such airports as Gloucestershire (Staverton) and Coventry, but although the flights were operated for a couple of seasons, eventually they were suspended.

A more recent enterprise has been the setting up of the Historic Flight. This operates a number of vintage aircraft including a DH Rapide, Avro Anson C21, Percival Prentice and Pembroke, an Autocrat and a Scottish Aviation Twin Pioneer, several being available

Above:
G-AMPZ — Douglas DC-3 of Air Atlantique/Atlantic Airlines.

Above:
G-SIXC — Douglas DC-6A of Atlantic Cargo/Atlantic Airlines.

for pleasure flights from Coventry. A passenger-carrying DC-3 usually attends the major UK air shows where it provides an opportunity for some local flying.

Above:
G-APRS — SA Twin Pioneer of Atlantic Airlines.

FLEET:
(ATLANTIC AIRLINES):

Regn	Series	C/n
Cessna 402B		
G-NOSE	-	0823
Cessna F406		
G-LEAF	-	0018
G-TURF	-	0020
Cessna 500 Citation		
G-LOFT	-	0331
Douglas DC-3		
G-AMPZ	C-47B	32872
G-AMRA	C-47B	26735
Douglas DC-6A		
G-APSA	–	45497
G-SIXC	-	45550
Fairchild Metro III		
G-BUKA	SA227C	AC-706B
Lockheed L188 Electra		
G-LOFA	CF	2002
G-LOFB	CF	1131
G-LOFC	CF	1100
G-LOFD	CF	1143
G-FIJR	PF	1138

(HISTORIC):
Auster J/1 Autocrat		
G-JAYI	-	2030
Avro 652A Anson		
G-VROE	C21	3634
DH89A Rapide		
G-AIDL	-	6968
Percival P40 Prentice		
G-APJB	-	PAC/084
Percival P66 Pembroke		
G-BXES	-	PAC/W/3032
Scottish Aviation Twin Pioneer 3		
G-APRS	-	561
G-AZHJ	-	577

(RECONNAISSANCE):
BN-2A Islander		
G-BCEN	26	403
Cessna 404 Titan		
G-EXEX	-	0037
G-TASK	-	0829
Douglas DC-3		
G-AMCA	C-47B	32966
G-AMHJ	C-47B	13468
G-AMPY	C-47B	26569
G-AMSV	C-47B	32820

(STORED):
Douglas DC-3		
G-AMPO	C-47B	33185
G-AMYJ	C-47B	32716

Aurigny Air Services (GR/AUR)

Head Office: States Airport, La Planque Lane, Forest, Guernsey, Channel Islands
Tel: (01481) 66444   Fax: (01481) 66446

For the past 30 years Aurigny has been providing inter-island air services plus links with southern England and northern France. When the venture started in March 1968 two Islanders comprised the fleet, but by 1970 traffic had increased to such an extent that eight of the nine-seat machines were needed to cope with the busy schedules. It soon became apparent that a larger capacity aircraft was needed, the solution being provided by Britten-Norman in the early 1970s. By inserting two fuselage plugs and the installation of an engine on top of the fin, it was possible to accommodate 17 passengers and one pilot. The result became the Trislander, the first example entering service with Aurigny in July 1971. Subsequently the airline has become the world's largest operator of the type which is ideal for the operations carried out.

While the oldest machine still has several years left before it has accumulated the prescribed 70,000 landings, the company has already begun to consider a suitable replacement for the sturdy tri-motor. This is by no means an easy task since almost all new types are turbine-powered which are prohibitively expensive to operate on such short sectors. An attempt to modernise the fleet with a slightly larger type was made as long ago as 1980 by introducing a pair of Twin Otters. These were not really satisfactory for the network, so after a couple of years or so both left the airline which promptly replaced them with more Trislanders.

Nevertheless, the company does have one turboprop type on strength, namely a Short SD3-60 which was acquired in 1990. This machine is used for some of the short inter-island schedules at peak times, but is mainly employed for passenger and cargo flights involving longer sectors. Aurigny's Royal Mail contract has been renewed on several occasions and involves the 360 flying a round trip between Jersey and East Midlands via Gatwick on five nights per week. The airline also carries mail and newspapers into Alderney and between Guernsey and Jersey.

There was a surprising development in 1987 when Aurigny purchased Guernsey Airlines from British Air Ferries. The latter had been operating a large number of schedules and charters into the islands from numerous UK regional airports but had encountered financial problems, hence the need to sell its subsidiary. Nevertheless, after the sale was completed, the new owner dropped all of the services, which included a link between

Above:
G-OAAS — Short SD3-60 Variant 100 of Aurigny Air Services.

Southampton and Jersey/Guernsey. With the reorganisation of some of the UK's domestic airlines in early 1998, interest in the Channel Islands' routes was shown by Aurigny, coupled with a report that it was considering an ATR-42 to replace the SD3-60 which is approaching the end of its spar life.

Although the carrier has remained profitable, there has been a decline in passenger numbers during the past few years due to competition from the sea ferries, particularly those to northern France. In order to produce some more revenue, Aurigny has repainted some of the Trislanders with special liveries advertising various companies in return for sponsorship. It is intended that at least half of the fleet, including the SD3-60, will remain in the traditional yellow livery.

FLEET:

Regn	Series	C/n
BN-2A Trislander		
G-BDTN	III-2	1026
G-BDWV	III-2	1035
G-BEPH	III-2	1052
G-BEPI	III-2	1053
G-BEVT	III-2	1057
G-JOEY	III-2	1016
G-OCTA	III-2	1008
G-RBSI	III-2	1027
G-XTOR	III-2	1065
Short SD3-60		
G-OAAS	100	SH3648

BAC Express Airlines (RPX)

Head Office: BAC House, Bonehurst Road, Horley, Surrey RH6 8QG
Tel: (01293) 821621   Fax: (01293) 821204

BAC Aircraft was formed in September 1992 as a wholly owned company within the BAC Group, adopting the revised title of BAC Express in January 1994. Its operations have subsequently involved contract passenger and freight operations, particularly for the Royal Mail, Parcel Force and other overnight courier companies. During the summer months passenger IT flights are operated from a number of regional airports to the Channel Islands, the departure points often being Cardiff, Southend, Southampton, Liverpool and Luton.

BAC Express is also available to operate scheduled flights on behalf of other carriers either short of capacity or needing cover for maintenance periods. In early 1998 these have included the Isle of Man-Dublin service for British Regional and the Exeter-Birmingham link for Jersey European. A mixed fleet of Friendships and Short SD3-60s is operated, although only the latter are suitable for quick changes of configuration from passenger to freight. The Dutch-built type is capable of carrying some 6 tonnes of freight, roughly double that of the 360s. More Friendships are due to join the fleet during 1998, with at least one equipped for passenger work. With such varied activities it not surprising that the aircraft are based as far apart as Belfast, Cardiff, Edinburgh, Exeter, the Isle of Man and Southend.

FLEET:

Regn	Series	C/n
Fokker F-27 Friendship		
G-BVOB	500	10366
G-BVZW	500	10425
G-JEAD	500	10627
G-	500	-
Short SD3-60		
G-CEAL	300	SH3761
G-CLAS	200	SH3635
G-ISLE	100	SH3638
G-KBAC	100	SH3758
G-LEGS	100	SH3637
G-OCEA	300	SH3762
G-OJSY	100	SH3603
G-VBAC	300	SH3736

Above:
G-CLAS — Short SD3-60 Variant 200 of BAC Express. Geoffrey P. Jones

Britannia Airways (BY/BAL)

Head Office: London Luton International
Airport, Luton, Bedfordshire LU2 9ND
Tel: (01582) 424155   Fax: (01582) 458594

The Luton-based airline can trace its history back to 1 December 1961 when a new British charter company was formed as Euravia (London) Ltd. It was closely associated with Universal Air Tours, a travel company that had been organising overseas holidays to the Mediterranean area for many years. The air travel arrangements had been entrusted to several airlines operating from Gatwick, but two had experienced financial and licensing difficulties during the year and had been forced to cease trading. Not surprisingly this affected the tour company which had to quickly find alternative carriers for the season. This unwelcome experience convinced Universal that it would be a wise move to form its own in-house airline.

During the winter of 1961/2 the company evaluated a number of types before eventually deciding to acquire a fleet of Constellations for operations from Luton. The first of Euravia's aircraft was delivered on 12 April 1962 whereupon some intensive crew training and route proving was begun to enable the first revenue-earning charter to be flown to Palma on 5 May, in this instance using Manchester as the UK departure point. Later in the year the airline took over Skyways which brought more Constellations and some Yorks into the fleet, although the latter continued their freighting duties with the new owner. By this time Euravia had widened its coverage of European destinations and had also increased the number of UK airports served. Such was the growing popularity of the IT holiday market, that it was apparent that the Constellations were becoming too small for the work and that a larger type was urgently needed.

Fortuitously BOAC had just retired its Bristol Britannia 102 fleet, most of which was parked at Cambridge pending sale. Euravia acquired a number of the turboprop airliners, taking the opportunity to change the airline's name to Britannia Airways shortly before the first aircraft was delivered in November 1964. On 6 December the first holidaymakers were flown from Luton to Tenerife, a destination that has become extremely popular through the years. In the following April, the airline was acquired by the Thomson Organisation which brought much experience and marketing skills to the carrier.

By 1968 Britannia Airways was flying clients of assorted tour operators which produced the need for yet more capacity. Subsequently the company became the second European operator of the Boeing 737, the first of which arrived at Luton on 8 July 1968. Initially the new aircraft were equipped with the same number of seats as the Britannias (117) which gave a degree of flexibility to the scheduling process, but this figure was increased to 124 in 1969 and to 130 two years later. It was December 1970 before the popular turboprop type was finally withdrawn leaving Britannia Airways with an all-jet fleet. There was a short-lived period between 1971 and 1973 when affinity group charters were attracting much attention. A couple of Boeing 707s were introduced and regularly flew the long-haul sectors to the US west coast with full loads until the market suddenly collapsed.

Thereafter the 737 fleet steadily increased in size to reach 14 in 1975, a year in which the airline carried some 2 million passengers. By 1983 this total had reached 4.4 million with the help of 29 Boeing 737s, but steps were already being taken to introduce a larger type to cope with this constant expansion. After considering the Airbus products, the TriStar and DC-10, the airline opted for the twin-aisle Boeing 767. The first two examples were delivered in 1984, with others arriving to form a fleet of six in 1988. By this time a start had been made on the gradual phasing out of the 737s, but it was not until 1994 that the last specimen left Britannia. In the meantime the company had absorbed Orion Airways in 1988 which added a number of the more advanced 737-300s to the collection, but it was decided to dispose of this variant because in the long term the carrier needed a larger type.

Eventually it was the narrow-bodied Boeing 757 that entered service in some numbers to become the mainstay of the fleet. These are backed up by the 767s which also maintain

Above:
G-OBYB — Boeing 767-304ER of Britannia Airways.

the long-haul services across the Atlantic and to Australia.

The departure of the 737s brought an end to Britannia's scheduled service between Luton and Belfast International which had proved popular with Irish travellers. Strangely, although the route was taken over by Emerald European, it was not a success and was quietly dropped. Similarly, Britannia had provided regular flights to and from Germany under contract to the MoD for some years. These were used for the movement of military personnel and their families, but it was thought that the 757 was too large for the purpose. Consequently the contract was awarded to British World which thereafter flew the sectors with a BAe 146.

For many years Britannia remained the favourite carrier amongst the travelling public, but towards the end of the 1980s it appeared that its position was in danger. Several of the new charter carriers, Air 2000 in particular, were setting standards that were quickly appreciated by the passengers. Any complacency was soon dispelled by Britannia's management which realised that a greater effort was needed, together with the introduction of new features such as in-flight entertainment.

The airline launched a new venture in mid-1997 when it formed a German subsidiary to compete with LTU and Condor. Known as Britannia GmbH, the newcomer began operations on 3 November using a Boeing 767-300ER transferred from its British parent. This is used for long-haul services to a number of Caribbean destinations, for the tour operator FTi Flights, using seven departure points in Germany. The coverage was intended to be expanded with the delivery of a second 767 in May 1998, to be followed by a further six in due course. A similar development was announced by Britannia in early 1998 which involved the takeover of Blue Scandinavia, the charter element of Transwede. In this case the company (to be known as Britannia AB) also operates 757s which have been repainted in the UK carrier's livery.

Above:
G-BYAD — Boeing 757-204 of Britannia Airways.

Above:
G-BYAB — Boeing 767-204ER of Britannia Airways.

FLEET:

Regn	Series	C/n
Airbus A320 (leased from TransAer 1998)		
EI-TLF	231	476
EI-TLH	231	247
EI-TLJ	231	257
Boeing 737 (leased from Sterling European)		
OY-SEE	3Y0	24463
Boeing 757		
G-BXOL	23A	24528
G-BYAD	204	26963
G-BYAE	204	26964
G-BYAF	204	26266
G-BYAG	204	26965
G-BYAH	204	26966
G-BYAI	204	26967
G-BYAJ	204	25623
G-BYAK	204	26267
G-BYAL	204	25626
G-BYAM	2T7	23895
G-BYAN	204	27219
G-BYAO	204	27235
G-BYAP	204	27236
G-BYAR	204	27237
G-BYAS	204	27238
G-BYAT	204	27208
G-BYAU	204	27220
G-BYAW	204	27234
G-	204	28834
Boeing 767		
G-BNYS	204ER	24013
G-BOPB	204ER	24239
G-BRIF	204ER	24736
G-BRIG	204ER	24757
G-BXOP	3S1ER	25221
G-BYAA	204ER	25058
G-BYAB	204ER	25139
G-OBYB	304ER	28040
G-OBYD	304ER	28042
G-OBYE	304ER	28979
G-OBYF	304ER	28883
G-OBYG	304ER	28884

(G-OBYA/YC transferred to Britannia GmbH)

British Airways (BA/BAW)

Head Office: PO Box 10, Speedbird House, London Heathrow Airport, Hounslow, Middlesex TW6 2JA
Tel: (0181) 759 5511   Fax: (0181) 562 9930

The national airline was established on 1 April 1972 to take control of both British Overseas Airways Corporation (BOAC) and British European Airways Corporation (BEAC). In addition to the main constituent parts, a number of subsidiaries were also involved in the reorganisation, including BEA Airtours, BEA Helicopters, Northeast Airlines and Cambrian Airways. For a time these companies displayed their individual identities on the aircraft, but it was not long before all traces were removed. As with all nationalised industries, the mergers brought a number of problems in the early days, but these have long since been overcome to produce a flag carrier which is respected around the world as a leading international airline. At present British Airways serves some 175 destinations spread around 75 countries, but the totals vary as new routes are added and others dropped from the network.

In 1980 the airline decided to end its involvement in most of its domestic operations to concentrate on the international business, although it retained the sectors between Heathrow and Edinburgh, Glasgow, Manchester and Belfast for a frequent shuttle service. The takeover of British Caledonian in 1987 gave BA a greater presence at Gatwick, which was further strengthened with the demise of Dan-Air in October 1992.

A new venture began in August 1993 when the first franchise agreement was signed with CityFlyer. Since that date more of the UK's smaller carriers have been enlisted to carry BA's livery including British Mediterranean, British Regional, GB Airways, Loganair and Maersk Air Ltd, plus the overseas companies Sun-Air and Comair. As a wholly-owned subsidiary, Brymon also flies with its parent's colours and flight numbers, but otherwise operates independently. The scheme has proved to be profitable for the participants, with significant increases in passenger figures recorded.

In recent years BA has taken a shareholding in TAT European which is now 100% owned, Air Liberté (67%), Deutsche BA (49%) and Air Mauritius (12.77%). Since acquiring these companies, operations have been reorganised to provide greater efficiency and less duplication. Elsewhere BA had a relationship with US Airways for some years, but this was not particularly beneficial to either partner. It is hoped that it will be replaced with an alliance with American Airlines, but in early 1998 this still had to receive the seal of approval from the authorities.

The national carrier has begun to replace its early Boeing 737-200s to meet the forthcoming noise regulations, with examples of the Series 300s joining the regional fleet as temporary replacements. In the longer term there will need to be substantial orders placed for aircraft in the 150-seat range to allow service entry from 1999. Meanwhile eight Series 300s, formerly operated by Philippine Airlines, were leased for the new low-cost carrier identified initially as Operation Blue Sky in late 1997. Based at Stansted, the airline was expected to start operations in the spring of 1998 to a number of European destinations. This latest venture has been carefully monitored by airlines such as Debonair and easyJet to ensure that the BA subsidiary is not being subsidised by its parent. They can be satisfied that their operations must have had an effect upon the flag carrier's activities to produce the need for competition.

FLEET:

Regn	Series	C/n
Airbus A320		
G-BUSB	111	006
G-BUSC	111	008
G-BUSD	111	011
G-BUSE	111	017
G-BUSF	111	018
G-BUSG	211	039
G-BUSH	211	042
G-BUSI	211	103
G-BUSJ	211	109
G-BUSK	211	120
BAe/Aérospatiale Concorde		
G-BOAA	102	206
G-BOAB	102	208

G-BOAC	102	204	G-BGDR	236	21805
G-BOAD	102	210	G-BGDT	236	21807
G-BOAE	102	212	G-BGJE	236	22026
G-BOAF	102	216	G-BGJF	236	22027
G-BOAG	102	214	G-BGJH	236	22029
BAe ATP			G-BGJJ	236	22031
G-BTPA	-	2007	G-BKYA	236	23159
G-BTPC	-	2010	G-BKYB	236	23160
G-BTPD	-	2011	G-BKYC	236	23161
G-BTPE	-	2012	G-BKYE	236	23163
G-BTPF	-	2013	G-BKYF	236	23164
G-BTPG	-	2014	G-BKYG	236	23165
G-BTPH	-	2015	G-BKYH	236	23166
G-BTPJ	-	2016	G-BKYI	236	23167
G-BTPO	-	2015	G-BKYJ	236	23168
G-BUWP	-	2053	G-BKYK	236	23169
Boeing 737			G-BKYL	236	23170
G-BGDA	236	21790	G-BKYM	236	23171
G-BGDB	236	21791	G-BKYN	236	23172
G-BGDE	236	21794	G-BKYO	236	23225
G-BGDF	236	21795	G-BKYP	236	23226
G-BGDG	236	21796	G-BSNV	4Q8	25168
G-BGDI	236	21798	G-BSNW	4Q8	25169
G-BGDJ	236	21799	G-BUHJ	4Q8	25164
G-BGDK	236	21800	G-BVNM	4S3	24163
G-BGDL	236	21801	G-BVNN	4S3	24164
G-BGDO	236	21803	G-BVNO	4S3	24167

Above:
G-BOAA — Concorde of British Airways.

Above:
G-BEBM — Douglas DC-10-30 of British Airways.

G-DOCA	436	25267	G-OFRA	36Q	29327
G-DOCB	436	25304	G-OHAJ	36Q	29141
G-DOCC	436	25305	G-OMUC	36Q	29405
G-DOCD	436	25439	G-XBHX	36N	28572
G-DOCE	436	25350	G-XMAN	36N	28573
G-DOCF	436	25407	**Boeing 747**		
G-DOCG	436	25408	G-AWNA	136	19761
G-DOCH	436	25428	G-AWNB	136	19762
G-DOCI	436	25839	G-AWNC	136	19763
G-DOCJ	436	25840	G-AWNE	136	19765
G-DOCK	436	25841	G-AWNF	136	19766
G-DOCL	436	25842	G-AWNG	136	20269
G-DOCM	436	25843	G-AWNH	136	20270
G-DOCN	436	25848	G-AWNJ	136	20272
G-DOCO	436	25849	G-AWNL	136	20284
G-DOCP	436	25850	G-AWNM	136	20708
G-DOCR	436	25851	G-AWNN	136	20809
G-DOCS	436	25852	G-AWNO	136	20810
G-DOCT	436	25853	G-AWNP	136	20952
G-DOCU	436	25854	G-BBPU	136	20953
G-DOCV	436	25855	G-BDPV	136	21213
G-DOCW	436	25856	G-BDXA	236B	21238
G-DOCX	436	25857	G-BDXB	236B	21239
G-DOCY	436	25844	G-BDXC	236B	21240
G-DOCZ	436	25858	G-BDXD	236B	21241
G-GBTA	436	25859	G-BDXE	236B	21350
G-GBTB	436	25860	G-BDXF	236B	21351
G-OAMS	37Q	28548	G-BDXG	236B	21536
G-ODUS	36Q	28659	G-BDXH	236B	21635

G-BDXI	236B	21830	G-BNLV	436	25427
G-BDXJ	236B	21831	G-BNLW	436	25432
G-BDXK	236B	22303	G-BNLX	436	25435
G-BDXL	236B	22305	G-BNLY	436	27090
G-BDXM	236B	23711	G-BNLZ	436	27091
G-BDXN	236B	23735	G-CIVA	436	27092
G-BDXO	236B	23799	G-CIVB	436	25811
G-BDXP	236B	24088	G-CIVC	436	25812
G-BNLA	436	23908	G-CIVD	436	27349
G-BNLB	436	23909	G-CIVE	436	27350
G-BNLC	436	23910	G-CIVF	436	25434
G-BNLD	436	23911	G-CIVG	436	25813
G-BNLE	436	24047	G-CIVH	436	25809
G-BNLF	436	24048	G-CIVI	436	25814
G-BNLG	436	24049	G-CIVJ	436	25817
G-BNLH	436	24050	G-CIVK	436	25818
G-BNLI	436	24051	G-CIVL	436	27478
G-BNLJ	436	24052	G-CIVM	436	28700
G-BNLK	436	24053	G-CIVN	436	28848
G-BNLL	436	24054	G-CIVO	436	28849
G-BNLM	436	24055	G-CIVP	436	28850
G-BNLN	436	24056	G-CIVR	436	25820
G-BNLO	436	24057	G-CIVS	436	28851
G-BNLP	436	24058	G-CIVT	436	25821
G-BNLR	436	24447	G-CIVU	436	25810
G-BNLS	436	24629	G-CIVV	436	25819
G-BNLT	436	24630	G-CIVW	436	25822
G-BNLU	436	25406	G-CIVX	436	28852

Below:
G-BKYB — Boeing 737-236 of British Airways. *AST Photography*

G-CIVY	436	28853	G-BIKH	236	22179
G-CIVZ	436	28854	G-BIKI	236	22180
Boeing 757			G-BIKJ	236	22181
G-BIKA	236	22172	G-BIKK	236	22182
G-BIKB	236	22173	G-BIKL	236	22183
G-BIKC	236	22174	G-BIKM	236	22184
G-BIKD	236	22175	G-BIKN	236	22186
G-BIKF	236	22177	G-BIKO	236	22187
G-BIKG	236	22178	G-BIKP	236	22188

Above:
G-ZZZD — Boeing 777-236 of British Airways.

G-BIKR	236	22189	G-BMRJ	236	24268
G-BIKS	236	22190	G-BPEA	236	24370
G-BIKT	236	23398	G-BPEB	236	24371
G-BIKU	236	23399	G-BPEC	236	24882
G-BIKV	236	23400	G-BPED	236	25059
G-BIKW	236	23492	G-BPEE	236	25060
G-BIKX	236	23493	G-BPEF	236	24120
G-BIKY	236	23533	G-BPEI	236	25806
G-BIKZ	236	23532	G-BPEJ	236	25807
G-BMRA	236	23710	G-BPEK	236	25808
G-BMRB	236	23975	G-CPEL	236	24398
G-BMRC	236	24072	G-CPEM	236	28665
G-BMRD	236	24073	G-CPEN	236	28666
G-BMRE	236	24074	G-CPEO	236	28667
G-BMRF	236	24101	G-CPEP	2Y0	25268
G-BMRG	236	24102	G-CPER	236	29113
G-BMRH	236	24266	**Boeing 767**		
G-BMRI	236	24267	G-BNWA	336ER	24333

Above:
G-VIIA — Boeing 777-236 of British Airways. *AST Photography*

G-BNWB	336ER	24334	G-VIIA	236IGW	27483
G-BNWC	336ER	24335	G-VIIB	236IGW	27484
G-BNWD	336ER	24336	G-VIIC	236IGW	27485
G-BNWE	336ER	24337	G-VIID	236IGW	27486
G-BNWF	336ER	24338	G-VIIE	236IGW	27487
G-BNWG	336ER	24339	G-VIIF	236IGW	27488
G-BNWH	336ER	24340	G-VIIG	236IGW	27489
G-BNWI	336ER	24341	G-VIIH	236IGW	27490
G-BNWJ	336ER	24342	G-VIIJ	236IGW	27492
G-BNWK	336ER	24343	G-VIIK	236IGW	28840
G-BNWL	336ER	25203	G-VIIL	236IGW	-
G-BNWM	336ER	25204	G-VIIM	236IGW	-
G-BNWN	336ER	25444	G-VIIN	236IGW	-
G-BNWO	336ER	25442	G-VIIO	236IGW	-
G-BNWP	336ER	25443	G-ZZZA	236	27105
G-BNWR	336ER	25732	G-ZZZB	236	27106
G-BNWS	336ER	25826	G-ZZZC	236	27107
G-BNWT	336ER	25828	G-ZZZD	236	27108
G-BNWU	336ER	25829	G-ZZZE	236	27109
G-BNWV	336ER	27140	**Douglas DC-10**		
G-BNWW	336ER	25831	G-BEBL	30	46949
G-BNWX	336ER	25832	G-BEBM	30	46921
G-BNWY	336ER	25834	G-BHDH	30	47816
G-BNWZ	336ER	25733	G-BHDI	30	47831
G-BZHA	336ER	-	G-BHDJ	30	47840
G-BZHB	336ER	-	G-DCIO	30	48277
G-BZHC	336ER	-	G-MULL	30	47888
Boeing 777			G-NUIK	30	46932
G-RAES	236IGW	27491			

British International Helicopters (BS/BIH)

Head Office: Buchan Road, Aberdeen Airport, Dyce, Aberdeen AB2 0BZ
Tel: (01224) 771353   Fax: (01224) 771632

The company was a subsidiary of British Airways until September 1986 when it was sold to SDR Helicopters. Scheduled passenger services between Penzance and the Scilly Isles had begun in September 1964, replacing the fixed-wing operations until the advent of Skybus in 1987. The helicopter sorties have subsequently continued, with the resident Sikorsky S-61 shuttling backwards and forwards throughout the day, although there are no services on Sundays. However, much of the carrier's effort is directed into the provision of support and charter services for the off-shore oil and gas rigs in the North Sea. BIH is now an operating subsidiary of the Canadian Helicopter Corporation.

FLEET:

Regn	Series	C/n
AS332L Super Puma		
G-BKZE	-	2102
G-BKZG	-	2106
G-BKZH	-	2107
G-BOZK	-	2179
G-BSOI	-	2063
G-BUZD	-	2069
G-BWHN	-	2017
G-TIGZ	-	2115
Sikorsky S-61N		
G-ATBJ	-	61269
G-ATFM	-	61270
G-AYOM	-	61143
G-AYOY	-	61476
G-BCEA	-	61721
G-BCEB	-	61454
G-BEDI	-	61754
G-BEIC	-	61222
G-BEJL	-	61224
G-BEOO	-	61771
G-BEWM	-	61772
G-BFFJ	-	61777
G-BFFK	-	61778
G-BSVO	-	61823

British Mediterranean Airways (KJ/LAJ)

Head Office: 53 Mount Street, Mayfair, London W1X 5RE
Tel: (0171) 493 3030   Fax: (0171) 493 9944

For many years the unrest in the Lebanon restricted air services to those of Middle East Airlines, but the end of the civil war enabled other carriers to offer flights to the Middle East country. One of these was British Mediterranean Airways which was formed specifically for this purpose. After the necessary approval had been received from the UK authorities, the airline took delivery of an Airbus A320 configured in a three-class 126-seat layout, which was followed by the award of the airline's Air Operator's Certificate (AOC).

The first scheduled service between Heathrow and Beirut was flown on 28 October 1994, but it was not long before the newcomer was involved in a disagreement with the CAA about the number of flights it could operate each week. In the meantime British Airways had announced its intention to resume its links with the Lebanon, but on a twice-weekly frequency. Since the agreement between the two countries permitted a total of only seven sorties, this meant that BMed was limited to five. Little progress was made to overcome this decision, so the airline introduced services to Amman and Damascus, the capital cities of Jordan and Syria respectively.

In September 1996 it was announced that BMed was to become the latest BA franchise, with the flag carrier ending its loss-making Middle East services that had been reinstated 18 months earlier. Meanwhile, BMed continued its operations with its A320 preparing to be repainted in BA livery, while two more examples of the type were ordered to cope with the planned route expansion. However, only one week before the agreement was due to be implemented, the negotiations were prematurely ended because

Above:
G-MEDD — Airbus A320-231 of British Mediterranean Airways. *AST Photography*

BA was not satisfied that its new partner could meet all the terms of the franchise agreement. Eventually such problems were overcome, with the result that British Mediterranean became a franchise in April 1997.

FLEET:

Regn	Series	C/n
Airbus A320		
G-MEDA	231	480
G-MEDB	231	376
G-MEDD	231	386

British Midland Airways
(BD/BMA)

Head Office: Donington Hall, Castle Donington, Derbyshire DE74 2SB
Tel: (01332) 854000   Fax: (01332) 854662

Although British Midland can trace its origins back to the prewar company Air Schools, it was not until 1949 that it was decided to expand into the commercial scene. It led to the creation of Derby Aviation which began to undertake passenger and freight charters from its base at Burnaston, Derby. This activity was developed in 1953 when the company applied for, and was granted, a licence to operate scheduled services to the Channel Islands with a Rapide. The seasonal service proved to be very popular and was therefore repeated in 1954, but with additional departure points.

In 1959 Derby Airways was formed, taking over all of the services and other activities of Derby Aviation. By this time these were being flown by DC-3s which also provided the opportunity for longer range sorties into Europe. In addition to the schedules, the airline also undertook IT charter flights, which were greatly expanded from 1961 following the arrival of three former BOAC Canadair Argonauts. These remained active until 1967 when one of the trio suffered a fatal crash on approach to Manchester. In those days there was a distinct reduction in demand during the winter months, so the fleet was employed on numerous freight charters in the slacker periods. Nevertheless, Derby Airways' passenger work was largely responsible for its success, with services operated from a number of airports including Birmingham, Bristol, Cardiff, Derby and Manchester.

In April 1965 East Midlands Airport was formally opened with British Midland Airways (BMA) becoming its first airline resident, the new name having been chosen to reflect its association with the region. By this time BMA had already acquired its first turboprop type, the forerunner of several Heralds used for charter and scheduled work. However, Viscounts were far more numerous, the fleet including seven bought from South African Airways, but in the meantime the carrier had entered the jet age with three new BAC One-Elevens. These were intended for some of the schedules, but in reality it was mainly the ITs that were expanded with contracts obtained from a number of tour operators. These used Luton, Belfast, Glasgow and Manchester as departure points in the early 1970s, but by 1972 BMA found that the charter market was uneconomic so it withdrew from the scene to concentrate on its scheduled work. The same decision was taken with the long-haul transatlantic flights operated at a loss for affinity group charters with Boeing 707s.

From this point BMA's scheduled network began to grow, introducing new routes with Viscounts and Heralds. Towards the end of the 1970s BMA revived its interest in jet-powered types, but this time selecting the DC-9 as its equipment. A number of specimens joined the airline at intervals to become the mainstay of the scheduled fleet until the advent of the Boeing 737 in 1987. The airline has subsequently continued to update its fleet since 1993 by adding three Fokker 70s, four Fokker 100s and eight Boeing 737-500s on lease from SAS. In July 1997 the company ordered its first Airbus product by signing a contract for 11 A320s and nine A321s, with deliveries due to start in the spring of 1998. Meanwhile a code-sharing agreement with Lufthansa was introduced from May 1997 between Heathrow, Cologne/Bonn and Rome, with Dresden replacing the Italian capital for the winter season's schedules.

Nowadays British Midland is a member of the Airlines of Britain Group which was restructured in February 1997 to avoid any

Above:
G-OBMY — Boeing 737-59D of British Midland Airways.

Above:
G-BVJD — Fokker 100 of British Midland Airways.

Below:
G-BVTE — Fokker 70 of British Midland Airways.

Below right:
G-GNTJ — SAAB 340 of Business Air/British Midland Airways. *A. S. Wright*

confusion with the BA franchise companies. As a result, British Regional, Business Air and Manx Airlines were transferred to British Regional Airlines (Holdings) Ltd, thereby ending the association with BMA.

FLEET:

Regn	Series	C/n
Airbus A320		
G-MIDF	231	-
G-MIDI	231	-
G-MIDJ	231	-
G-MIDN	231	-
G-MIDO	231	-
G-MIDP	231	-
G-MIDS	231	-
G-MIDT	231	-
G-MIDU	231	-
G-MIDV	231	-
Airbus A321		
G-MIDA	231	806
G-MIDB	231	810
G-MIDC	231	835
G-MIDE	231	-
G-MIDH	231	-
G-MIDK	231	-
G-MIDL	231	-
G-MIDM	231	-
G-MIDR	231	-
G-MIDW	231	-
Boeing 737		
G-BVKA	59D	24694
G-BVKB	59D	27268
G-BVKC	59D	24695
G-BVKD	59D	26421
G-BVZE	59D	26422
G-BVZF	59D	25038
G-BVZG	5Q8	25160
G-BVZH	5Q8	25166
G-BVZI	5Q8	25167
G-ECAS	36N	28554
G-OBMD	33A	24092
G-OBMH	33A	24460
G-OBMJ	33A	24461
G-OBMP	3Q8	24963
G-OBMR	5Y0	25185
G-OBMX	59D	25065
G-OBMY	59D	26419
G-OBMZ	53A	24754
G-ODSK	37Q	28537
G-OJTW	36N	28558
G-SMDB	36N	28557
G-OBMF	4Y0	23868
G-OBMG	4Y0	23870
G-OBMM	4Y0	25177
G-OBMO	4Q8	26280
G-SFBH	46N	28723
Fokker 70		
G-BVTE	-	11538
G-BVTF	-	11539
G-BVTG	-	11551
Fokker 100		
G-BVJA	-	11489
G-BVJB	-	11488
G-BVJC	-	11497
G-BVJD	-	11503

British Regional Airlines
(BABRT)
Head Office: Isle of Man (Ronaldsway) Airport, Ballasalla, Isle of Man IM9 2JE
Tel: (01624) 826000   Fax: (01624) 826001

British Regional Airlines (BRA) was known as Manx Airlines (Europe) until the new name was adopted on 1 September 1996. There had already been considerable reorganisation in 1994 when Loganair's operations were reduced in size so that the carrier could concentrate on its Scottish services. Following this development, it did not need such types as the ATP and Jetstream 41 for these activities, so they were transferred to Manx (Europe), while the latter's Short SD3-60s joined the Glasgow-based company. New operating bases were set up at Edinburgh and Southampton by Manx (Europe), which became a British Airways franchise in January 1995. Its fleet of 25 aircraft was duly repainted to portray its new status which involved flying to 22 destinations within the UK and mainland Europe. However, all operations involving flights to and from the Isle of Man remained with Manx Airlines. Early in 1996 the latter took over Loganair's BA franchise commitments as part of its expansion which continued with the acquisition of a pair of ex-Knight Air Jetstream 31s together with the company's routes to Aberdeen and Southampton.

In October 1996, the newly formed British Regional assumed responsibility for BA's unprofitable Highlands and Islands services, necessitating the return of two ATPs serving with British Midland and the lease of a SAAB 340 from Business Air to cover the Aberdeen-Orkney services. Loganair left the group in February 1997 after a management buy-out, the new company successfully bidding for the Scottish air ambulance services with a Twin Otter and four Islanders.

In the meantime British Regional had been evaluating suitable jet equipment, eventually ordering three Embraer RJ145s. The first of the 50-seat type entered service on the Manchester-Berlin route in August 1997, to be followed by operations from Southampton when the next machine was delivered. BRA has now signed a letter of intent for a further 10 models plus five options, the first of the latest batch having been due to join the fleet in early 1998. The RJ145s will gradually replace the turboprop fleet on UK services.

FLEET:

Regn	Series	C/n
BAe ATP		
G-BRLY	-	2025
G-MANE	-	2045
G-MANF	-	2040
G-MANG	-	2018
G-MANH	-	2017
G-MANJ	-	2004
G-MANL	-	2003
G-MANM	-	2005
G-MANP	-	2023
G-MAUD	-	2002
BAe Jetstream		
G-MAJB	4102	41018
G-MAJC	4102	41005
G-MAJD	4102	41006
G-MAJE	4102	41007
G-MAJF	4102	41008
G-MAJG	4102	41009
G-MAJH	4102	41010
G-MAJI	4102	41011
G-MAJJ	4102	41024
G-MAJK	4102	41070
G-MAJL	4102	41087
G-MAJM	4102	41096
BAe 146		
G-MANS	200	E2088
G-GNTZ	200	E2036
Embraer RJ145		
G-EMBA	-	145016
G-EMBB	-	145021
G-EMBC	-	145024
G-EMBD	-	039
G-EMBE	-	042
SAAB 340		
G-GNTE	-	133
Short SD3-60		
G-BKMX	100	SH3608
G-BLGB	100	SH3641
G-BMAR	100	SH3633
G-ISLE	100	SH3638
G-LEGS	100	SH3637
G-WACK	100	SH3611

Above:
G-MAJD — BAe Jetstream 41 of British Regional Airlines/BA Express.

Below:
G-MAUD — BAe ATP of British Regional Airlines.

British World Airlines
(VF/BWL)
Head Office: Viscount House, Southend Airport, Essex SS2 6YL
Tel: (01702) 344435   Fax: (01702) 331914

British World was officially formed on 6 April 1993, yet it was able to celebrate its 50th anniversary in November 1996. This claim was justified as a direct descendant of Silver City Airways which was formally registered in 1946. Although one of many postwar newcomers, unlike the majority it had the advantage of possessing a board of directors with a wide experience of company affairs. It also differed in the choice of aircraft which were not the usual recently-demobbed types, but three factory-fresh Avro Lancastrians, the civil version of the Lancaster bomber. These were used for a couple of years to provide a link with Australia, but the airline is better known for its association with the Bristol Freighter and the car ferry industry. The company introduced regular services across the English Channel in the late 1940s, which rapidly became an extremely popular alternative to sea travel. Throughout the next two decades Silver City carried thousands of cars and passengers from the UK to France and later beyond, changing its name to British United Air Ferries on 1 January 1963.

Prior to this development it had already been decided that a replacement type was necessary for the ageing Freighters, eventually leading to the Carvair, an ingenious conversion of the Douglas DC-4. The first examples of the new aircraft entered service in the spring of 1962 in time to meet the healthy demand on the newly inaugurated services to more distant European destinations. At the same time the Freighters broke all records on the traditional sectors, but quite suddenly the situation changed, with plans for expansion replaced by schemes for contraction as loads steadily declined. This was largely due to the fact that the sea ferry companies were now employing ships designed for the purpose, at the same time offering highly competitive fares.

There was little that the airline could do to reverse the trend, although the air ferry services continued to operate into the 1970s, albeit on a much reduced scale. A change of name to British Air Ferries (BAF) in October 1967 merely brought some administration economies, so it was with some urgency that the airline sought ideas for survival. Since there was no shortage of travellers prepared to leave their cars at home, it was decided to operate some of the schedules on a passenger-only basis. A Viscount was leased from Aer Lingus for two seasons, with a pair of HS748s joining it for the second period until November 1971.

A change of owner produced new ideas including a brief encounter with the Canadair CL-44 which it was thought could replace the Carvair. In the event, the type quickly proved unsuitable, leaving its predecessor to be refurbished in an attempt to revive the car ferry business. However, eventually the airline was forced to accept that this mode of transport was no longer commercially viable. Nevertheless, it was early 1975 before any permanent replacement arrived at Southend in the shape of a Handley Page Herald, the first of three acquired from Canada. After overhaul the type took over BAF's regular cross-Channel schedules, although the traffic figures did not encourage any immediate expansion. This lack of growth convinced the airline that leasing was a more profitable undertaking than commercial services, so it was decided that more Heralds would be sought. In due course almost all of the available survivors of the breed found their way back to Southend where they were quickly overhauled ready for service with various customers around the world. It was certainly a less demanding occupation than running the schedules, so the latter aspect of BAF's business was transferred to British Island Airways from 1 January 1979.

Undoubtedly, had more Heralds been forthcoming, BAF would have added them to the fleet to keep pace with the demand. Fortunately, at this time British Airways had decided to retire its Viscount fleet which offered an ideal opportunity to acquire some of these well-maintained and inexpensive aircraft. By the summer of 1982 the carrier had 18 of the popular turboprops on strength, initially for both leasing and charter work. Within a year there was another change of ownership, this time bringing a return to the scheduled service and passenger charter market. In the meantime Guernsey Airlines had been bought, bringing with it the main trunk route between Guernsey and London.

Above:
G-OBWL — BAe ATP of British World Airlines.

From the mid-1980s, BAF enjoyed considerable success with the airline flying schedules and charters to the Channel Islands from 14 regional airports. However, probably the most important expansion came in April 1985 when the Southend-based carrier launched its first international service to link Gatwick with Rotterdam. At first the route showed great promise, but this quickly evaporated as the competing airlines forced fares down beyond an economic level. BAF persevered for two years but it was eventually forced to end the operation.

Undaunted, the company began frequent low-fare services between Southampton and the Channel Islands in April 1987. A record number of advance bookings were received which seemed to confirm that neither the public nor the travel trade was in favour of complicated and restrictive fare structures. Unfortunately, problems within the company forced some rapid contractions with the Southampton link an early casualty. The company then came under the administration of chartered accountants in January 1988, while operations were restricted to existing contract charters for such companies as Shell and Virgin Atlantic. With the help of this successful trading, BAF became the first major British company to emerge from administration under the 1986 Insolvency Act.

It was not long before the airline entered into the jet age, albeit with three elderly BAC One-Elevens, two of which were used for charter work. A more modern type in the shape of a BAe 146 joined the growing fleet in 1991 for charter work on behalf of the smaller tour operators, but it was towards the end of 1992 that there was an opportunity to expand this type of business. The takeover of Dan-Air by British Airways removed a considerable amount of capacity from the market since the flag carrier had no interest in acquiring more One-Elevens. As a result, the 11-strong fleet was ferried to Southend for storage, with five aircraft earmarked for service with BAF. This proved to be a temporary stage because on 6 April 1993 the company changed its name to British World Airlines (BWA). During the year the airline enjoyed a surge in the holiday market which kept the fleet fully occupied, so it came as a surprise when the airline announced it intended to launch a scheduled service between Stansted and Bucharest in June, a strange destination to choose, but one felt to have potential. Unfortunately the expected growth failed to materialise, so the venture was ended in the spring of 1994.

There were no more forays into the scheduled market, the airline preferring instead to use the five One-Elevens for charter work or to supply additional capacity and support to other airlines as required. BWA was also awarded a valuable contract from the Ministry of Defence (MoD) for the movement of service personnel and their families between the UK and various bases in Germany. At first a 146 was employed for the regular work, but due to the escalating leasing charges for this type, BWA returned the aircraft to British Aerospace and substituted a One-Eleven for the MoD flights.

Throughout the period, the remaining members of the Viscount fleet had been employed to fulfil nightly mail contracts and the regular flights between Aberdeen and Sumburgh for Shell UK. Sadly, in 1996 the time arrived for the type to be finally withdrawn from passenger work and replaced by a pair of ATR72-210s, the first new aircraft ever bought by the airline. During the course of 1997 all of the active Viscount freighters were gradually taken out of service as the various contracts expired, many of the surviving airworthy aircraft being sold in South Africa. In fact, the distinction of making the last Viscount landing in the UK went to G-AOHM when it arrived at Southend on 8 January 1998 after a flight from Belfast. A new type was added to the fleet in the latter part of 1997 when the first of two BAe ATPs was delivered for freight and passenger work. These will be joined by two more in 1998 with others following if the venture proves a success.

Other activities undertaken by the airline include the operation and support of aircraft flown by start-up carriers. In 1996 BWA began this task for the Luton-based newcomer Debonair until the latter obtained its own Air Operator's Certificate. A similar role was played for Classic Airways, a company that planned to offer back-up facilities with a TriStar.

Below:
G-OBWB — BAC One-Eleven 518FG of British World Airlines.

Opposite:
G-OILA — Aérospatiale ATR-72-210 of British World Airlines. *British World*

FLEET:

Regn	Series	C/n
Aérospatiale ATR-72		
G-OILA	210	472
G-OILB	210	473
BAC One-Eleven		
G-OBWA	518FG	232
G-OBWB	518FG	202
G-OBWC	520FN	230
G-OBWD	518FG	203
G-OBWE	531FS	242
BAe ATP		
G-OBWL	-	2057
G-OBWM	-	2058
G-OBWN	-	-
G-OBWO	-	-

Brymon Airways (BRY)

Head Office: Plymouth City Airport, Crownhill, Plymouth, Devon PL6 8BW
Tel: (01752) 705151   Fax: (01752) 793067

When Brymon Aviation was formed in 1969, its intended role was to offer flying training at Fairoaks. These activities were expanded in the following year with the acquisition of an Islander for general charter work, some of this involving the movement of shellfish from Cornwall to France. During the summer season the aircraft was also used for pleasure flying from Land's End (St Just), with trips to the Scilly Isles included from time to time. Since these proved to be popular, Brymon decided to convert the sorties into scheduled services in June 1972 using Newquay (St Mawgan) as the mainland terminal. In addition, the Islander also flew over the Newquay-Plymouth-Jersey route at weekends, with any spare time spent with charter flights.

At the end of 1972 Brymon had carried some 2,500 passengers and had added another Islander to the fleet to cope with this volume of traffic. It had also been necessary to relocate the airline's headquarters to Plymouth where there was greater scope for expansion. The following year brought more growth, with the company planning to operate 35 scheduled flights per week with the help of network extensions to Guernsey, Exeter and Morlaix in northern France. It proved to be another successful period, with a total of 9,000 customers for Brymon Airways' flights, the title now used by the company as its trading name.

There was a significant event in 1974 when Brymon became the first UK carrier to operate the DHC Twin Otter, with more of the STOL type joining the fleet during the next few years. Traffic figures continued to climb annually as new services were introduced, one particularly important addition being the Heathrow-Newquay sector which was taken over from British Midland and flown by a Herald several times per day. Throughout the remainder of the 1970s Brymon further consolidated its position as the West Country's airline, confirmed in 1979 when an unprecedented 85,000 travellers used the services.

There was a major fleet change in August 1981 when the company's first DHC Dash Seven was delivered, a type ideally suited to the compact conditions at Plymouth. Initially the new airliner was allocated to the support required by the oil-related industry in the Shetlands, but with the arrival of another two examples by the end of the year, Brymon was able to extend the Heathrow route to Plymouth, leaving two aircraft to maintain the Scottish contracts.

Meanwhile the possibility of building an airport on the now-disused docklands area in East London was being investigated by John Mowlem & Co. By the nature of the locality, any facility would be limited in size, which in turn would restrict the types able to operate from the airport. The project interested Brymon Airways which gave a considerable boost to the project in 1982 when it carried out an impressive demonstration by landing one of its Dash Sevens at Heron's Wharf on the Isle of Dogs. It proved the viability of the enterprise and convinced the public and politicians that the environment would not suffer. Brymon subsequently played a large part in the development of what has become London City Airport, rightfully making history on 27 October 1987 when Dash Seven G-BRYC landed with the first revenue-earning service to open the airport for business.

Even before this event, Brymon had been granted a 125-year lease on Plymouth which encouraged the airline to upgrade the airport with hard runways and a brand-new terminal building. Towards the end of the 1980s it had been decided to introduce the twin-engined Dash Eight to the fleet, to some extent replacing the Dash Seven. The first of the newcomers was delivered in October 1990 to be followed by examples of both the Series 100 and 300 variants. Two years later, in October 1992, it was announced that Brymon Airways was to merge with Birmingham European Airways, the resulting company trading as Brymon European.

Above:
G-BRYJ — DHC-8-311 Dash Eight of Brymon Airways/BA.

This arrangement lasted only a year before the decision was taken to separate the two airlines again with BA assuming full ownership of Brymon, while its previous partner came under the control of Maersk Air Ltd.

At this point Brymon's name disappeared from the aircraft after a repaint into the flag carrier's full livery and titles. It seemed strange that BA should be interested in the operations of its latest acquisition, which left the valuable Heathrow slots held by the company as the main attraction. These were used for the popular Plymouth-London service which consistently enjoyed high load factors as an essential link with the southwest. Happily the transfer was smoothly accomplished, with BA intimating that it intended Brymon to continue as a separate company.

During its first year with BA the traffic figures increased dramatically as the commercial and marketing benefits took full effect. This trend subsequently continued with a modernised fleet equipped entirely with Dash Eight 300s, which now cover scheduled flights from Aberdeen, Bristol, Cork, Edinburgh, Gatwick, Glasgow, Newquay, Newcastle, Paris, Southampton and the Channel Islands. However, two Dash Sevens were transferred to a new subsidiary known as Brymon Offshore Air Charter which operates the machines for oil-related duties from its Aberdeen base. Interestingly, on 30 March 1997 a long-expected action was taken by BA when it moved the London terminal of Brymon's Plymouth service to Gatwick.

FLEET:

Regn	Series	C/n
DHC-7 Dash Seven		
G-BRYA	110	062
G-BRYD	110	109
DHC-8 Dash Eight		
G-BRYI	311	256
G-BRYJ	311	319
G-BRYK	311	284
G-BRYM	311	305
G-BRYO	311	311
G-BRYP	311	315
G-BRYR	311	336
G-BRYS	311	296
G-BRYT	311	334

Business Air (II/GNT)

Head Office: Kirkhill Business House, Howemoss Drive, Dyce, Aberdeen AB2 0GL
Tel: (01224) 401900   Fax: (01224) 770141

Until Business Air was formed in July 1987, Scottish carriers had not enjoyed sustained success through the years. The newcomer absorbed the interests of Euroair and Business Air Centre and was formally launched with the benefit of the British Airways financial package designed to help independent airlines establish domestic services. Three Bandeirantes were inherited with the purchase which were used for charters and night mail work, but the company was well aware of the dangers of relying on one source for its income. Therefore steps were taken to add scheduled services to its activities as soon as possible.

On 7 April 1988 the airline introduced a link between Aberdeen and Esbjerg, a Danish city with similar oil-related interests to its Scottish counterpart. The Bandeirante employed also called at Dundee, where commercial services had never caused much congestion in the past. Although the route was primarily intended for business travellers, it soon became popular for leisure purposes, with the Danes appreciating the opportunities for hunting and fishing expeditions.

Two months or so after the start of the international service, Business Air received the CAA's approval to take over the Aberdeen-Dundee-Manchester route, resulting in the lease of the Short SD3-60 G-OJSY from Jersey European. As the airline cautiously expanded, it realised that it was essential to modernise the fleet with a type designed for relatively short-sector operations. Of the types on offer, the SAAB 340 appeared to be most promising, so Business Air approached Basle-based Crossair, the type's launch customer in the early 1980s. The Swiss carrier had already amassed considerable experience which convinced the UK company that the 340 would meet its demands. Crossair was also sufficiently impressed by Business Air's plans to take a

15% stake in July 1990.

The new association also provided the source of the Scottish airline's first 340A (G-GNTA) because the Swiss operator was already seeking homes for the older variant as its new Series B machines were delivered. Arriving in September 1990, it immediately took over the scheduled services, although these alone were insufficient to produce a satisfactory utilisation figure. It was therefore highly desirable that the 340 was also employed on the night mail work, but this was only practical with Quick Change (QC) capability. After rejecting a costly conversion offered by the manufacturer, Business Air opted for a cheaper but adequate scheme involving a simple modification to the rear bulkhead to give easy access to the cabin. Seats could then be removed through the rear door in some 20min, followed by the fixing of plywood panels to protect the interior of the cabin.

In June 1992 Business Air added the Aberdeen-Edinburgh-East Midlands route to its network, by which time it had four 340s on strength enabling two to be dedicated to the new venture. Although in competition with Aberdeen Airways, the carrier was confident that the introduction of the modern equipment would not have a detrimental effect upon the fortunes of its rival. In fact, after barely two months, Business Air found itself alone on the route following the sudden demise of Aberdeen Airways. Consequently the service began to produce some impressive support from the public, which was met by increasing the frequency until five return trips per day where flown by mid-1993.

During August the airline signed a marketing and code-sharing agreement with Lufthansa, the main feature being the introduction of flights between London City and Frankfurt. Furthermore, a hub was established at Manchester to synchronise schedules of both carriers to provide better connections for passengers. The German service from the Docklands airport was flown by a BAe 146-200 leased from Crossair, the aircraft night-stopping at Frankfurt to give German-originating traffic an early morning departure. For some time the 146 retained its Swiss identity, but eventually it was repainted in Business Air livery with the UK registration G-GNTZ. Meanwhile, the German flag carrier had acquired a 38% stake in the Scottish airline, later in September 1994 assuming full commercial responsibility for the year-old Frankfurt route. The same 146 remained in use but was now wet-leased from Business Air, an arrangement that continued until 1997 when one of Lufthansa's Avro RJ85s took over the duties. Relieved of its commitments at London City, the displaced aircraft was transferred to British Regional for use on BA's Inverness-Gatwick scheduled service.

A year earlier, Business Air had become wholly-owned by the Airlines of Britain Group which promised better opportunities for expansion, together with various wet-leasing contracts. Neither Crossair nor Lufthansa retained any financial interest at this point, although the commercial co-operation continued. The latest arrangement allowed Business Air to develop its own routes between Scotland and Manchester, with particular emphasis on transfer traffic. Further restructuring took place in the spring of 1997 when the airline became a part of British Regional Airlines (Holdings) Group. The change brought the need for more equipment expansion, so by the end of the year Business Air had increased its fleet size to 11 SAAB 340s. These took over more of British Midland's operations at Leeds/Bradford and East Midlands, resulting in most of the

FLEET:

Regn	Series	C/n
SAAB 340		
G-GNTA	A (QC)	049
G-GNTB	A (QC)	082
G-GNTC	A (QC)	020
G-GNTD	A (QC)	100
G-GNTE	A (QC)	133
G-GNTF	A (QC)	113
G-GNTG	A (QC)	126
G-GNTH	B	169
G-GNTI	B	172
G-GNTJ	B	192
G-RUNG	A	086

Business Air operates a number of SAAB 340s for British Midland. G-GNTE is flown in BA livery.

machines being repainted in the latter's livery. Interestingly, one of the 340s (G-GNTE) was wet-leased to British Regional Airlines to operate British Airways' services between Aberdeen, Shetland and Orkney, for which it was given the flag carrier's new colour scheme. However, it did not involve Business Air becoming a BA franchise. Future fleet changes could result in at least three 50-seat SAAB 2000s joining the fleet in 1998.

Caledonian Airways (KG/CKT)

Head Office: Caledonian House, Gatwick Airport, Crawley, West Sussex RH6 0LF
Tel: (01293) 668280   Fax: (01293) 668353

Caledonian Airways was originally formed in April 1961 to provide long-haul charter services, particularly to the US. Initially, Douglas DC-7s were employed, but these were gradually replaced by Britannias in the mid-1960s. Towards the end of the decade Caledonian decided to add BAC One-Elevens to its fleet for European IT flights, mainly using Gatwick, Manchester and Glasgow as departure points. In 1970 the airline took over British United Airways, the combined companies becoming British Caledonian Airways.

Meanwhile British European Airways had formed a subsidiary company in 1969 known as BEA Airtours specifically to handle IT charters from Gatwick. Comets transferred from the parent company formed the initial fleet, but by the end of 1973 the type had been replaced by a number of former BOAC Boeing 707s. These were kept busy on IT flights covering all parts of southern Europe, the Canary Islands and North Africa, with Manchester departures added to the Gatwick operations. A major change was introduced on 1 April 1974 when British Airways was formally established by merging the interests of BEA and BOAC. Naturally this also affected the charter subsidiary, so thereafter it adopted the title of British Airtours. By 1980 the ageing 707s were in the process of being replaced by the more efficient 737, a type that became the mainstay of the fleet.

There was another reshuffle of airlines and equipment in 1988 when British Caledonian became a wholly-owned subsidiary of British Airways, in so doing merging its own charter activities with those of British Airtours. The new airline revived the name Caledonian Airways and inherited a mixed fleet of Boeing 737s, 757s and Lockheed TriStars to maintain the short- and long-haul IT services.

Below:
G-BBAJ — Lockheed L1011 TriStar 100 of Caledonian Airways.

This remained the situation until December 1994 when British Airways sold the company to the Inspirations Group, a transaction that included five TriStars and the use of some 757s and DC-10s in order to fulfil the outstanding contracts held by the carrier. In addition, the three Airbus A320s already ordered by Inspirations were delivered in time for the 1995 summer programme. There was yet another change of ownership in September 1997 when the Chairman (Eammon Mullaney) took a majority interest in the company with the remaining shares acquired by the Carlton Leisure Group. The airline plans to increase its capacity by leasing two former Dragonair A320s in May 1998.

FLEET:

Regn	Series	C/n
Airbus A320		
G-BVYA	231	354
G-BVYB	231	357
G-BVYC	231	411
G-CVYD	231	393
G-CVYE	231	394
Douglas DC-10		
G-GOKT	30	47838
G-LYON	30	47818
Lockheed L1011 TriStar		
G-BBAE	100	1083
G-BBAF	100	1093
G-BBAH	100	1101
G-BBAI	1	1102
G-BBAJ	100	1106
G-CEAP	50	1145

Above:
G-BVYA — Airbus A320-231 of Caledonian Airways.

Channel Express
(Air Services) (LS/EXS)

Head Office: Building 470, Bournemouth International Airport, Christchurch, Dorset BH23 6SE
Tel: (01202) 593344   Fax: (01202) 573512

The Bournemouth-based company began operations in 1978 as Express Air Services with a small fleet of Handley Page Heralds. These were employed on frequent cargo flights to the Channel Islands, with freshly-cut flowers often comprising the cargo for the return trip to the south coast airport. At an early stage in the airline's career it employed the Heralds for weekend passenger work over the same routes in the summer season, but this activity was soon discontinued.

After obtaining some Post Office contracts for the nightly movement of mail, more examples of the type were obtained from various sources until eight were operated for the regular work and ad hoc charters. In the early 1990s a modernisation programme was instigated to uprate and refurbish most of the fleet to so-called Super Herald standard, an undertaking that significantly improved the performance of the aircraft. Although the type continued to serve the airline faithfully for some years, eventually it was necessary to consider a replacement. From the mid-1990s there was therefore a gradual phasing-out process in favour of the Fokker F-27 Friendship 500/600 which is faster, complies with the Stage 3 night-time noise regulations and has a payload of some 15,000lb (6,800kg). Nevertheless, it was expected it would be the latter part of 1998 before the last Herald (G-BEYF) was finally withdrawn thereby ending the type's 20 years' service with the airline.

A need for more capacity over a longer range was responsible for Channel considering a larger type in the late 1980s. This led to the introduction of several Lockheed Electras that had been converted for freight duties in the US after their passenger-carrying careers had ended some years earlier. The modifications included the installation of a forward cargo door 11ft 3in x 6ft 11in (343cm x 211cm) giving the Electras compatibility with the wide-bodied types. Channel employs its aircraft on both domestic and international sectors, the containerised loads allowing much faster turn-rounds, an all-important feature of night mail and parcel operations.

During 1997 Channel took delivery of its first Airbus A300B4 after its conversion by BAe Aviation Services at Bristol/Filton. Although certification was expected in May, the necessary approval was not received until late summer, whereupon the aircraft was able to start regular flights between Tel Aviv and Stansted on behalf of British Airways, in addition to charter work for a number of other companies. It was soon apparent that the early choice of the type as an ideal medium-sized freighter was fully vindicated and was encouraging other carriers to follow the lead. In the meantime, Channel announced that it would be introducing a second example in February 1998, followed by a third in May.

The airline still flies between its Bournemouth base and the Channel Islands, but also includes Bristol, Coventry, East Midlands, Edinburgh, Gatwick, Liverpool, Luton, Newcastle and Stansted in its coverage.

FLEET:

Regn	Series	C/n
Airbus A300B4		
G-CEXC	103F	124
G-CEXH	203F	117
G-	203F	121
Fokker F-27 Friendship		
G-BNIZ	600	10405
G-CEXB	500	10550
G-CEXD	600	10351
G-CEXE	500	10654
G-CEXF	500	10660
G-CHNL	600	10508
G-JEAP	500	10459
Handley Page Herald		
G-BEYF	401	175
Lockheed Electra		
G-CEXS	L188CF	1091
G-CHNX	L188AF	1068
G-OFRT	L188CF	1075

(G-JEAP leased from JEA. Electras N341HA, N343HA and N360Q leased occasionally)

Left top:
G-CEXF — Fokker F-27-500 of Channel Express.
Channel Express

Left middle:
G-CEXC — Airbus A300B4-103F of Channel Express.
A. S. Wright

Left bottom:
N360Q — Lockheed L188 Electra of Channel Express.
A. S. Wright

CityFlyer Express (FD/CFE)

Head Office: Iain Stewart Centre, Beehive Ring Road, Gatwick Airport, West Sussex RH6 0PB
Tel: (01293) 567837   Fax: (01293) 567829

The airline was originally formed as Connectair in 1982 with a single Bandeirante acquired from Air Ecosse. Most of the carrier's activities initially involved scheduled trips between Gatwick and Antwerp, which were later flown as a member of British Caledonian Commuter. In early 1986 the route network was expanded with the addition of a Rotterdam service, for which purpose a Short SD3-30 was introduced. After being acquired by the International Leisure Group, the name Air Europe Express was adopted by the airline in February 1989, at the same time adding Düsseldorf to the scheduled coverage.

Although the company successfully operated the feeder services for its parent, the collapse of the latter in March 1991 also brought the subsidiary's activities to a halt. However, after a month or so a management buy-out meant that the airline was able to start again, albeit now known as Euroworld. At first the operations were restricted to regular night freight sorties, but regional passenger services were restarted in August 1991 with its leased SD3-60s. Another name change took place in February 1992 when the present title was adopted, but this became less obvious in August 1993 when the company began flying as a British Airways franchise. All scheduled services have subsequently been operated using the flag carrier's flight codes, with the aircraft carrying BA livery and titles.

CityFlyer became the first UK operator of the ATR-42 and ATR-72 in April 1992 and October 1994 respectively, later repeating this example by becoming the first UK carrier to employ the Avro RJ100 in 1997. Two specimens were delivered in the spring, with a further three planned to enter service by June 1998. The franchise arrangement has proved highly successful for CityFlyer which achieved its best ever financial year and carried a record number of passengers in 1996/7. Much of this was due to the introduction of the RJs which were responsible for tremendous growth on the Dublin and Amsterdam routes. In addition to these two sectors, CityFlyer/BA currently flies schedules from Gatwick to a further 11 European destinations including Antwerp, Bremen, Cologne/Bonn, Cork, Düsseldorf, Guernsey, Jersey, Leeds/Bradford, Luxembourg, Newcastle, Rotterdam and Zürich. Charters are

Below:
G-BXAS — Avro RJ100 of CityFlyer/BA Express. *International Airways*

also flown, particularly in the summer when several UK regional airports are linked with the Channel Islands.

FLEET:

Regn	Series	C/n
Aérospatiale ATR-42		
G-BUEA	300	268
G-BUEB	300	304
G-BVEC	300	356
G-BVED	300	315
G-BVEF	300	331
G-BXEG	300	329
Aérospatiale ATR-72		
G-BVTJ	202	342
G-BVTK	202	357
G-BWTL	202	441
G-BWTM	202	470
G-BXTN	202	483
Avro RJ100		
G-BXAR	-	E3298
G-BXAS	-	E3301
G-BZAT	-	E3320
G-BZAU	-	E3329
G-BZAV	-	E3332

Classic Airways (CCN)

Head Office: Bolney Place, Cowfold Road, Bolney, West Sussex RH17 5QT
Tel: (01444) 882188   Fax: (01444) 881123

Observing the airlines' growing need for short-term additional capacity or back-up assistance for aircraft suffering technical troubles, a group of investors together with the Independent Aviation Group formed Classic Airways in 1997. It had already been decided that there was a shortage of wide-bodied equipment available for such duties for which the Lockheed TriStar was considered eminently suited. There were also a number in store awaiting customers, so in due course an ex-Cathay Pacific machine was acquired and ferried back to the UK in July for overhaul and refurbishment by Marshall Aerospace at Cambridge.

British World was contracted to operate the machine on its Air Operator's Certificate, an airline that already specialised insuch activities with One-Elevens. In due course the necessary

Above:
G-IOII — Lockheed L1011 TriStar 100 of Classic Airways.

approval was obtained from the CAA enabling the first revenue-earning sortie to be flown.

At one point it had been expected that this would be possible in September, but in the event it was October before the inaugural commercial charter was operated between Newcastle and Palma as a back-up for Peach Air. When not in service, the 362-seat TriStar is based at Stansted where it was expected to be joined by a second example in February 1998, followed by a third in June.

FLEET:

Regn	Series	C/n
Lockheed L1011 TriStar		
G-IOII	100	1118
G-	100	-
G-	100	-

Debonair Airways (2G/DEB)

Head Office: 146 Prospect Way, London Luton International Airport, Luton, Bedfordshire LU2 9BA
Tel: (0541) 500147   Fax: (0541) 500147

The airline was created to provide low cost but high quality scheduled flights in Europe. Originally, Gatwick was chosen as its base, but at an early stage it was apparent that slot problems would make it difficult to maintain the service levels envisaged. With costs as an important consideration, a number of suitable alternative airports were carefully evaluated before choosing Luton as its hub and headquarters. Once this was settled the proposed route network was the next important detail to be resolved, with Amsterdam, Barcelona, Copenhagen, Munich and Newcastle chosen as the initial destinations. However, this selection was amended before operations began by dropping the Dutch airport since in the meantime it had become one of easyJet's routes and there was little point in competing with the rival carrier. Debonair therefore decided to substitute Düsseldorf Express, the upgraded regional airport at Mönchengladbach. Since it is much smaller and less congested than the city's main international facility, it provides the same type of service as Luton, with short distances between terminal and aircraft.

From the outset Debonair had opted for the BAe 146-200, a machine thought ideal for this type of operation. Negotiations resulted in seven aircraft being leased from USAir after spending several years in storage in the US. Refurbishment was carried out by Cambridge-based Marshall Aerospace which delivered two examples to Debonair before the start of commercial services. In accordance with its policy of being an innovator rather than an imitator, fares were set at a low level without jeopardising a high standard of comfort. Only beverages and light refreshments are provided, which is perfectly adequate for the sectors flown. In-flight entertainment is provided in all 96 seats with the equipment an integral part of the seat-back table. In addition to a variety of programmes, video games and casino-style gambling by using a credit card has been included.

On launch day, 19 June 1996, it was Düsseldorf Express, Munich and Barcelona that formed the network, the frequency of flights varying from one to three per day with one-way fares set at £39, £49 and £59. By 10 July it was possible to make some significant changes to the programme with revised times and new routes made possible by a third aircraft joining the fleet. A daily visit to Madrid was introduced together with an important domestic sector to Newcastle. The latter was thought to have great promise and revived a similar operation of the 1960s, but in the event it failed to receive sufficient support. The route was therefore reluctantly dropped in January 1997 after contributing to the airline's first-year loss of £16 million.

Debonair became the first UK airline to offer intra-European and fifth freedom flights within a single country's borders when services began between Munich and Düsseldorf and between Barcelona and Madrid, with load factors proving to be very encouraging. In August 1997 a new direct daily service linked Munich with Madrid, but in the following month the airline ceased the Rome-Barcelona and Copenhagen-Munich routes because neither operation was making an acceptable contribution. Debonair received its own operating certificate on 1 October, British World having previously been responsible for operations. A new commercial alliance with the Italian carrier Azzurra Air began in the same month, with the result that daily flights between London Luton and Milan Bergamo were started as a code-sharing venture. This was followed on 13 December by the UK carrier introducing a daily sortie to Nice, this time in competition with easyJet.

Despite a substantial increase in turnover, the airline still fell significantly short of the revenue targets for the 1997 peak summer season. There were a number of factors responsible including the late delivery of the sixth and seventh aircraft and an underestimation of the amount of advertising necessary to achieve the required level of summer bookings. It was accepted that the slacker winter months would not help the situation, especially since the five additional aircraft due to be leased were unlikely to be available until the beginning of the 1998 summer season.

There was a significant advance in the carrier's fortunes in early January when it was announced that a fourth hub was to be set up in southern Italy from 1 February with flights operating full time out of the Calabrian airports of Lamezia and Reggio to Turin, Bologna, Florence and Rome. A vast amount of traffic is expected to be generated by the construction of the world's longest road bridge between mainland Italy and Sicily plus the building of Europe's largest shipping port at Gioia Tauro. Debonair has an agreement with the Calabrian authorities for five years' minimum which should produce a big increase in revenue and yield to the airline.

FLEET:

Regn	Series	C/n
BAe 146		
G-DEBA	200	E2028
G-DEBC	200	E2024
G-DEBD	200	E2034
G-DEBE	200	E2022
G-DEBF	200	E2023
G-DEBG	200	E2040
G-DEBH	200	E2045
G-	300	E3191
G-	300	E3185
G-	300	E3181
G-	300	E3206
G-	300	E3189

Above:
G-DEBE — BAe 146-200 of Debonair Airways.

easyJet Airline (U2/EZY)

Head Office: Easyland, London Luton
International Airport, Bedfordshire LU2 9LS
Tel: (01582) 445566   Fax: (01582) 443355

Formed in October 1995 by Stelios Hajiloannou of the Greek shipping line Stelmar Tankers, commercial flying began one month later with a thrice-daily domestic service between its Luton base and Glasgow, although the frequency was reduced by one at weekends. The same arrangements applied when a second Scottish route was introduced two weeks later, this time Edinburgh being the destination. Initially a pair of Boeing 737-200s were leased from the International Aviation Group and operated by GB Airways, with Air Foyle later taking over the responsibility for all operations since easyJet still had to receive its Air Operator's Certificate (AOC) from the CAA. Aberdeen was added to the expanding network in due course, while Amsterdam became the airline's first international destination in the spring of 1996.

As the coverage was steadily expanded, so a growing shortage of aircraft began to create difficulties. By the spring of 1997 the two original 737-200s had been returned off lease and were already flying for Virgin Express, but the replacement Series 300s due to join the fleet had not arrived. Eventually one of the missing duo was delivered which certainly helped the situation, but it still meant that the company was trying to operate a network designed for five aircraft with only four. Delays were inevitable with some routes being more seriously affected than others. In an effort to reduce the size of the problem, easyJet decided to cut the frequencies on a number of sectors as a temporary measure in order to maintain its coverage during this unfortunate period.

Needless to say, would-be passengers were not particularly happy when arriving for a flight that had either been cancelled or was running some 2hr late. Aberdeen was particularly hard hit with its thrice-daily frequencies trimmed to a single rotation per day. In the short term it did not help the airline's reputation for reliability, but by midsummer the absent 737 joined the fleet thereby enabling full service to be restored. In fact, it was also possible to create a second

Above:
G-EZYD — Boeing 737-3M8 of easyJet Airline.

hub at Liverpool in October 1997 using a based 737-300 for scheduled flights to Amsterdam and Nice. Following this development easyJet began to plan a third hub, this time located in Scotland. In addition, the introduction of bases at Amsterdam and Athens together with routes to Cyprus and Jersey are likely to play a part in the carrier's European expansion.

Another 737 was acquired in November, by which time the airline had been awarded its own AOC by the CAA. Earlier easyJet had announced its longer term plans for the fleet which included an order for 12 737-300s from Boeing with deliveries starting in August 1998 and thereafter continuing at a rate of one per month for the next year. At this point it is forecast that the airline will be carrying six million passengers annually compared with 1.5 million in 1996. From these figures it can be appreciated that the concept of a no-frills, low-fares airline has won the support of travellers.

FLEET:

Regn	Series	C/n			
Boeing 737					
G-EZYA	3Y0	23498	G-	300	-
G-EZYB	3M8	24020	G-	300	-
G-EZYC	3Y0	24462	G-	300	-
G-EZYD	3M8	24022	G-	300	-
G-EZYE	3Q8	24068	G-	300	-
G-EZYF	375	23708	G-	300	-
G-	300	-	G-	300	-
G-	300	-	G-	300	-
G-	300	-	G-	300	-

Emerald Airways (G3/JEM)

Head Office: South Terminal, Liverpool Airport, Speke Hall Avenue, Merseyside L24 1YW
Tel: (0151) 448 0844   Fax: (0151) 448 0549

Prior to 1993, the airline traded as Janes Aviation with its headquarters located at Blackpool. It was formed on 1 December 1987; operations starting with an Islander employed on cargo work between its home airport and Belfast. Initially the flights were mainly on behalf of Lynx Express Delivery Network, but as the business expanded with other customers, so a Trislander and a pair of DC-3s joined the fleet to cope with the demand. The latter type was replaced after a brief time by a Short SD3-30 which proved a more efficient machine for the duties which involved regular flights across the Irish Sea to the Isle of Man, Belfast and Eire. For a period in the early 1990s two Heralds were also leased, but in late 1991 the airline began its acquaintance with the HS748. The first of the breed to be acquired was G-BPDA, a specimen that had previously been with Chieftain Airways and Scottish European, both short-lived Scottish carriers.

With the aircraft proving eminently suited to the cargo work envisaged, the company quickly began to collect more 748s from various sources around the world until they formed the largest fleet of the type in Europe. It enabled Janes to secure more valuable contracts, especially those covering the nightly movement of mail and parcels for the Post Office together with newspapers for clients of Reed Aviation.

In June 1993 the airline decided to move its base to Liverpool where it adopted the new title of Emerald Airways, a name chosen to reflect the amount of business carried out across the Irish Sea. It was not the first time that an airline had used this identity through the years, but none of the now-defunct carriers had any connection with the present company.

Approval was received in September 1994 for the airline to operate passenger flights with its 748s, of which 10 were on strength at this point. Two machines were reserved for the rapid transformation exercise, whereupon 48 seats could be installed when necessary. Nowadays there are three specimens that are frequently converted, while two are permanently configured for passenger duties. This became necessary with the introduction of scheduled flights between Liverpool and the Isle of Man in April 1996, together with ad hoc and contract charters. Meanwhile the company has continued with its mail work which involves regular visits to Leeds/Bradford and Stansted. Other sectors flown with cargo include Coventry-Belfast-Liverpool, a round trip between Belfast and Liverpool and a similar sortie from Dublin calling at Liverpool and Belfast before returning to the Irish capital. Emerald's 748s are also available for ad hoc cargo and passenger charters to destinations throughout Europe, with the possibility of more scheduled routes being launched in the future. Now fully established at Liverpool, the airline has its administration offices and engineering division based at the airport, although the Jersey European facility at Exeter is also used for some overhauls.

FLEET:

Regn	Series	C/n
HS748		
G-ATMI	2A	1592
G-ATMJ	2A	1593
G-AYIM	2A	1687
G-BEJD	1	1543
G-BGMO	2A	1767
G-BIUV	2A (SCD)	1701
G-BMFT	2A	1714
G-BPDA	2A	1756
G-BVOU	2A	1721
G-BVOV	2A	1777
G-EMRD	2B	1797
G-OJEM	2B	1791
G-OSOE	2A	1697
G-SOEI	2A	1689

Above:
G-EMRD — HS748 Srs 2B of Emerald Airways.

European Airways (L8/EAW)
Head Office: Diamond Court, Kingston Park, Newcastle upon Tyne, Northumberland NE3 2EN
Tel: (0191) 214 0299   Fax: (0191) 286 9938

Formed in 1994 with Uzbekistan Airways holding a 40% interest, the airline began operations on 27 February 1995. It was intended that a network of regional services would be built up from its Newcastle base with the first routes linking the northeast airport with Manchester and Southampton, Manchester with Exeter, and Southampton with Le Havre in northern France. In view of the ownership it was perhaps not surprising that a scheduled service to Tashkent was under consideration, but nearer home Barcelona and Hamburg were seriously evaluated but not introduced. Nowadays BCE Business Funding has a 20% interest in the company while the remaining 80% is held by private investors. Since the launch all services have been flown by a pair of BAe Jetstream 31s leased from Birmingham-based Maersk Air Ltd, although an association with Gill Airways is apparent by the use of the latter's flight codes for the schedules.

Below:
G-OBEA — BAe Jetstream 3102 of European Airways.

FLEET:
Regn	Series	C/n			
BAe Jetstream					
G-CBEA	31	609	G-OBEA	31	607

European Aviation Air Charter (EAF)
Head Office: European Aviation House, Bournemouth International Airport, Christchurch, Dorset BH23 6EA
Tel: (01202) 581111   Fax: (01202) 578383

After BA had withdrawn all of its BAC One-Eleven 510s from service in 1993, they were flown to Bournemouth pending disposal. Although a number of airlines showed an interest in the well-maintained machines, no sales were actually finalised. It was at this point that European Aviation (EAL) decided to acquire the entire fleet which now consisted of 16 Series 510s, two having already been allocated to the Duxford and Cosford museums by BA. It did not go unnoticed by the company that there was a steady reduction in the number of aircraft available in the 100-seat capacity range, a situation brought about by the demise of such airlines as British Island and Dan-Air. It was therefore decided to offer a leasing service to carriers in need of such an aircraft using the refurbished One-Elevens.

One of the first customers was the Air Bristol group which leased two machines, one to fulfil a regular contract and the second for back-up purposes and ad hoc charters. It was not long before European realised that it could expand its activities still further by undertaking such work in its own right. Accordingly EAL created European Aviation Air Charter (EAAC) in September 1993, which was followed by the granting of its Air Operator's Certificate (AOC) on 16 February 1994. Meanwhile, after an extensive maintenance programme, two members of the fleet (G-AVMH and 'MI) were repainted in the company's smart red and white colours in readiness for the planned operations. At that point the cabin interiors and seat covers remained largely unchanged from their BA days, but subsequently these have gradually been replaced by European. At the same time the total capacity has been increased from 94 to a standard 104 seats, a configuration which still provides ample leg-room for the passengers. Surprisingly, the ex-BA Series 510s were not equipped with forward airstairs, although in the wake of the British Caledonian merger the flag carrier later inherited specimens fitted with this useful feature. Four of these were duly added to the European fleet where they were found to be well suited to IT work, so in due course work began to bring the Series 510s to the same standard. There were also differences in the flightdeck layouts, often necessitating the retraining of crews before they were able to handle the 510s, especially since most of the pilots were recruited from Dan-Air in the early days.

Towards the end of 1994, European expanded its activities when it became involved in the scheduled service market. A 51% stake was taken in a new airline known as Emerald European, which was created in partnership with an Icelandic consortium to link Luton with Belfast International. Previously Britannia Airways had offered twice-daily Boeing 737 flights on the route, but with the withdrawal of the type, the company no longer had suitable equipment available. One of European's One-Elevens was therefore allocated to the duties when the schedules were introduced, although the aircraft retained its normal livery and titles. A low-fares policy was adopted at the outset, but business travellers were given the option of an upgraded service. However, despite early promise, by the following spring the Bournemouth-based company had decided to end its participation in the venture.

Following the signing of new contracts with a number of carriers, EAAC decided to increase the size of its operational fleet by three aircraft during 1995. This in turn produced the need for additional pilots, but by this time the traditional sources for recruitment were exhausted. There was therefore little alternative but to become the first airline for several years to recruit staff without a One-Eleven type rating, at the same time underwriting the cost of the conversion training. Twelve pilots were needed to meet the shortfall, all required to possess an Air Transport Pilot's Licence and a minimum of 2,000hr on jets, amassed either from commercial or military flying. Several hundred applications were received from which 17 were selected for interview before the final choices were made. After training, the newcomers were introduced as first officers and allocated to bases at Edinburgh, Gatwick, Glasgow, Manchester and Stansted. This influx of staff took EAAC's strength from eight to 24 flightdeck crews in just over a year, while in the same period cabin crews (each comprising three members) increased from seven to 24.

By this time European had moved its headquarters from Filton back to its birthplace at Hurn. A 4.86ha (12-acre) site was acquired from FLS, which included four hangars that had housed part of the original One-Eleven production line, so it was also a homecoming for most of the fleet. In addition to these buildings, further office accommodation was also taken over, enabling operations, marketing, training and general administration services to be housed. In due course a One-Eleven cabin trainer produced by the fuselage of the retired G-AVMJ was installed in one of the hangars, along with Boeing 727, TriStar and One-Eleven 510 simulators. Both of the trijet units are in demand by customers still operating the two

Below:
G-AVMP — BAC One-Eleven 510ED of European Aviation Air Charter.

types, which should keep the equipment busy for some years to come.

At an early stage in the airline's existence it had been decided to adapt one of the One-Elevens to meet the demands of the corporate market. The selected airframe was G-AZMF, a Series 530FX which had served with British Caledonian originally until taken over by BA in 1988. During the overhaul and conversion programme, the cabin interior was completely refurbished and the capacity reduced to 50 passengers. The luxury seats were installed two-abreast with a pitch of 47in (119cm) and equipped with foot-rests. Service entry came in January 1995 with a sortie for Nissan Cars involving a round trip between Gatwick and Lisbon. In fact, with a range of 1,250 nautical miles (2,316km), the One-Eleven is capable of reaching cities such as Athens with ease without the inconvenience of an intermediate stop. Subsequently the aircraft has been chartered by many organisations and individuals for flights which have taken it to a variety of destinations far and wide. European received sufficient business during its first year to encourage the conversion of a second aircraft, this time configured with a business class interior. In this case the same type of seats were installed in a two-abreast arrangement, but set at a 34in (86cm) pitch to increase the total capacity to 70 passengers.

This was thought likely to appeal to airlines seeking a suitably sized aircraft with which to develop new routes, but in the event the aircraft (G-AVMI) was chartered by Air Bristol to operate the daily British Aerospace air bridge between Filton and Toulouse.

Of course the company's ability to respond quickly and competitively with an ACMI package (aircraft, crew, maintenance and insurance) to airlines wishing to inject additional capacity at short notice, has brought increasing business. One-Elevens regularly fly for Ryanair and Air UK, while longer term contracts for airlines such as SABENA resulted in three aircraft operating for the Belgian flag carrier in 1995/6. Two were employed on the schedules linking Glasgow and Edinburgh with Brussels, while the third was flown in support of flights operated by Delta Air Transport. More recently, at the end of March 1997, Jersey European's livery was to be seen on One-Eleven G-AVMK when it took over the airline's Stansted-Belfast International schedules for the duration of the summer season, a contract later extended for the winter. The Bournemouth-based start-up carrier Euroscot began its regular links with Glasgow and Edinburgh in September 1997 having wet-leased a One-Eleven from European, while AB Airlines uses the same source for the equipment employed on its scheduled services. On its own account, in November 1997 European was awarded the MoD contract for the movement of military personnel and their families between the UK and Germany, work previously undertaken by British World.

Although a popular and reliable aircraft, unfortunately the One-Eleven certainly makes its presence heard, with all operators well aware that the type will be grounded in 2002 unless steps are taken to meet the Stage 3 noise regulations. European is no exception, so the company has evaluated various hush kits before reaching the decision to fund joint development with the Miami-based company Quiet Technologies Corporation (QTC).

The US manufacturer has already gained considerable experience during the development of hush kits for the Spey 511-powered Gulfstream 2 and 3, plus similar work on the engines of Boeing 707s and Douglas DC-8s. Components were shipped to QTC during 1997 to facilitate the assembly of a prototype proof-of-concept hush kit, which when completed was due to be dispatched to the UK in readiness for the early December start of about 30hr test flying. Carried out with the full co-operation of the CAA and British Aerospace, if the programme is completed successfully, then flight-testing of production units will continue until the anticipated certification date towards the end of 1998.

Parallel to this activity, a hush kit is in the process of development with the aim of reducing the noise output from the auxiliary power unit (APU). European is also planning to introduce a flightdeck upgrade for the fleet which will bring some useful commonality to the One-Elevens. Currently the aircraft are equipped with either Rockwell-Collins or Smiths Industries avionic systems, with the layout of the flightdeck depending upon the original customer's requirements. A 'glass cockpit' may replace the primary instruments in all the aircraft, a modernisation exercise which would certainly extend the type's operational career appreciably. Internally the One-Elevens are smarter than they have ever been following some major refurbishment and certainly stand any comparison with much younger and modern types in airline service today.

In the meantime, European added a number of airframes to its collection that were acquired from both the Argentine carrier Austral and Philippine Airlines. Most of them have been reduced to spares, but four were ferried to Bournemouth for storage with two earmarked for the hush kit trials. These are both ex-Austral machines which have exchanged their temporary Bermudan identities for the UK registrations G-HKIT and G-IIIH. Interestingly, the latter was an active member of the long-defunct Court Line fleet in the early 1970s when it carried the mark G-AXMF.

Despite European's obvious satisfaction with the One-Eleven, this has not prevented other types from being considered. One surprising addition to the fleet was the Boeing 727-51 OK-TGX which was acquired from the Czech airline Air Terrex. However, although repainted in EAAC's full colours, the machine was later sold to Balkh Airlines based in Afghanistan. In late 1997 European announced that it had purchased a pair of 28-year-old Boeing 737-200s from United Airlines, described by the company as a commercial opportunity and a significant development for the Group. No details were released about the intended use, but since the variant can equal the One-Eleven for noise levels attained, any potential customers would be outside Europe due to the restrictions on such aircraft. News was also released about the purchase of two former British Airways Boeing 747-100s, a number of ex-Air France Airbus A300s and 13 Boeing 737-200s due to be phased out by SABENA in 1999. All of these may be leased out, sold or reduced to spares.

FLEET:

Regn	Series	C/n
BAC One-Eleven		
G-AVMH	510ED	136
G-AVMI	510ED	137
G-AVMK	510ED	139
G-AVML	510ED	140
G-AVMM	510ED	141
G-AVMN	510ED	142
G-AVMP	510ED	144
G-AVMR	510ED	145
G-AVMS	510ED	146

G-AVMT	510ED	147	G-HKIT	521FH	196
G-AVMV	510ED	149	VP-BEA	524FF	195 (ex Philippine A/L)
G-AVMW	510ED	150			
G-AVMX	510ED	151	VP-BEB	527FK	226 (ex Philippine A/L)
G-AVMY	510ED	152			
G-AVMZ	510ED	153	**Boeing 737**		
G-AWYV	501EX	178	VP-BEE	222	19934
G-AXLL	523FJ	193	VP-BEF	222	19953
G-AYOP	530FX	233	**Airbus A300B2**		
G-AZMF	530FX	240	-	1C	027
G-IIIH	518FG	200			

Euroscot Express (MY/EUJ)

Head Office: Premier House, 111 Station Road, Edgware, Middlesex HA8 7BJ
Tel: (0181) 951 5656   Fax: (0181) 951 1556

After a lengthy incubation period, Euroscot finally began its operations on 29 September 1997 using a BAC One-Eleven leased from European Aviation. At one point in the planning stage the airline was considering the use of BAe 146s on routes from Scotland to London City and the European mainland, but these projects were dropped when Air UK began similar operations. After further research it was decided to operate from Bournemouth, an airport with excellent but underused facilities. Preparations were made to serve Glasgow on a daily basis and Edinburgh at weekends with one return flight on each of Friday, Saturday and Sunday. Since day returns are not possible with the launch frequency, it was the leisure market that was most likely to provide the majority of customers. With single fares set at £39 single plus government tax, within a month of start-up the service was exceeding all expectations with load factors reaching 50% instead of the 20% to 25% figure anticipated. The airline also devised a scheme with the Scottish City Link coach operator whereby passengers could avail themselves of return travel anywhere in Scotland for £5.

Within a short time the airline was considering a service to Amsterdam, following KLM's decision to end its association with the route between the Dutch city and Southampton. Euroscot hoped to acquire a second One-Eleven to permit a mid-January start for this operation, but since the type does not comply with the Stage 3 noise regulations, approval by the Netherlands

Below:
G-AVMT — BAC One-Eleven 510ED of Euroscot.

authorities seemed doubtful. Provisionally it was arranged that a 146 would be substituted as an interim measure until the results of the trials of the hush kit under development by European Aviation and Quiet Technologies for the One-Eleven were completed.

Longer term plans include the use of a number of Boeing 737s, but the company does not intend to expand too quickly since it is well aware of the failure rate of new carriers in the UK. Only too often the high investment commitments necessary proved too heavy a burden for them to manage. In this respect Euroscot was fortunate in having a founder, Mr Jack Romero, who had successfully launched British Mediterranean Airlines in 1994 in order to provide scheduled services to the Middle East with a single Airbus A320. In fact he remained a majority shareholder in the company which has become a British Airways franchise.

FLEET:

Regn	Series	C/n
BAC One-Eleven		
G-AVMT	510ED	147

Flightline (FLT)

Head Office: Viscount House, Aviation Way, Southend Airport, Essex SS2 6UN
Tel: (01702) 543000   Fax: (01702) 547778

Although based at Southend since it was formed in 1989, the airline's jet fleet operates from other UK airports. An ex-Dan-Air BAe 146-300 (G-BPNT) was acquired in 1993 and has subsequently been based at Bournemouth from where it flies IT charters on behalf of Palmair, an associate company of the tour operator Bath Travel. This activity was expanded in 1997 when the aircraft regularly visited Dundee with a Palma service during the summer programme, making a technical stop at Liverpool or Manchester on the return leg. The new terminal facilities at Southampton have encouraged greater use of the airport, with the result that ITs and short breaks were offered by Palmair to such places as Palma, Jersey, Prague and Venice. Normally at the end of the day's activities the 146 positioned back to Bournemouth.

Below:
G-OZRH — BAe 146-200 of Flightline.

Despite its relatively small size, in 1997 Palmair Flightline was acclaimed in *Holiday Which* as the fifth best airline in the world, ranking well ahead of many of the big and established carriers. The award was based on food, cleanliness, comfort/leg-room, in-flight entertainment and check-in staff.

Earlier in the year Flightline had operated a pair of 146s between Gatwick, Toulouse and Bordeaux under a wet-lease contract with British Airways. At the end of the specified period, one machine recommenced its work for Falcon Travel AG by operating regular charter flights from Stansted to Zürich, Geneva and Basle. The second was retained by BA for a time to enable the aircraft to fly on the routes between Gatwick, Aberdeen, Edinburgh and Glasgow. A similar requirement by Transavia during 1997 resulted in a 146 covering the airline's commitments on the busy Gatwick-Amsterdam route for the summer programme, for which purpose it carried the Dutch carrier's full livery.

FLEET:

Regn	Series	C/n
BAe 146		
G-BPNT	300	E3126
G-FLTA	200	E2048
G-OZRH	200	E2047
G-TBIC	200	E2025
Beech King Air		
G-FLTI	65-F90	LA-59
Embraer EMB-110 Bandeirante		
G-FLTY	P1	215
G-OFLT	P1	211

Below:
G-BPNT — BAe 146-300 of Palmair/Flightline. *A. S. Wright*

Flying Colours Airlines
(MT/FCL)
Head Office: Building 790, Terminal 2,
Manchester International Airport M90 4FX
Tel: (0161) 489 5757   Fax: (0161) 489 5758

The airline was established in November 1995 by the Flying Colours Leisure Group which also includes the tour operators Sunset Holidays, Priority Holidays and Club 18-30. Operations began in the spring of 1997 with four leased Boeing 757s carrying the Group's IT passengers. Three of the aircraft were based at Manchester with the fourth flying from Gatwick, the quartet all having transatlantic capability. Delivery of the first machine was made at the end of February followed by the second on 26 March in time for the inaugural flights. Although fleet expansion was already planned for 1998, such was the demand that the airline had to lease an Airbus A320 for the 1997 summer season exclusively for operations from Glasgow. The aircraft (G-BXAT) was delivered to the airline on 15 May and thereafter carried the Scottish customers to the familiar destinations in the sun until returned to the lessor in October for service with Air France. Two additional 757s were due to join the airline for the 1998 season.

Below:
G-FCLC — Boeing 757-28A of Flying Colours Airlines.

FLEET:

Regn	Series	C/n
Boeing 757		
G-FCLA	28A	27621
G-FCLB	28A	28164
G-FCLC	28A	28166
G-FCLD	25F	28718
G-FCLE	-	-

GB Airways (GT/GBL)
Head Office: Iain Stewart Centre, Beehive Ring Road South, Gatwick Airport, West Sussex RH6 0PB
Tel: (01293) 664239   Fax: (01293) 664218

Gibraltar Airways was formed towards the end of 1930 when the chairman of the Bland shipping line set up the company as a subsidiary. A Saro Windhover flying boat entered service on the route linking Gibraltar with Tangier, a venture that lasted only about two months before it was suspended. In the event it transpired that it was to be a lengthy period of non-activity because it was 15 May 1947 before the company was resurrected in association with BEA. The latter held 51% of the shares until February 1960 when Bland resumed control once again.

The airline, trading as Gibair, was created to restart the Tangier service which duly began on 30 August 1947 with DH Rapides, a type which continued the run until replaced on

5 October 1953 by DC-3s operated by BEA. In 1959 the equipment was upgraded to a Viscount seconded from the UK carrier's fleet, a procedure that ended in 1974 when the flag carrier bought a single Viscount 800 from New Zealand National Airways Corporation specifically for the use of Gibair. Registered G-BBVH and painted in the latter's livery, the machine remained the property of BEA until sold to its associate company in 1981. The aircraft's somewhat monotonous activities were brightened occasionally by operating charters to the Channel Islands and the UK. Sadly its career came to an end on 23 November 1988 when it was damaged beyond repair when landing at Tangier.

For many years the trunk route to the UK was operated from Heathrow by Tridents leased from BEA, but on 1 April 1979 Gibair moved its terminal to Gatwick and changed its equipment to a Boeing 737 leased from Britannia Airways. The airline modified its title to GB Airways on 1 November 1981, a name still in use although the source of its aircraft has changed through the years. Nowadays Boeing 737s are employed on services to Gibraltar, Madeira, Morocco and Tunisia using Gatwick, Heathrow and Manchester as the UK gateways. Additional destinations were planned for the 1998 summer season with schedules serving more North African airports together with Spain, Portugal, Malta and Mallorca. The older B737-200s were also due to be replaced by new Series 300 aircraft, each configured with 130 seats in a two-class arrangement.

FLEET:

Regn	Series	C/n
Boeing 737		
G-BNNK	4Q8	24069
G-BNNL	4Q8	24070
G-BUHL	4S3	25134
G-OGBA	4S3	25596
G-OGBB	34S	29108
G-OGBC	34S	29109
G-OGBD	3L9	27833
G-TREN	4S3	24796

Gill Airways (9C/GIL)

Head Office: New Aviation House, Newcastle International Airport, Newcastle upon Tyne NE13 8BT
Tel: (0191) 214 6600   Fax: (0191) 214 6699

The company began operations in January 1967 as Gill Aviation, its main occupation being flying training with a variety of types. Air taxi services were started in the late 1960s, with the expanding North Sea oil industry generating much business. During the 1970s Gill also operated a growing number of executive twin-engined machines for assorted companies in the area, but in the next decade the airline became increasingly involved in mail and freight contracts using its newly acquired Short SD-30s.

Passenger schedules were successfully started in 1989 under the title GillAir, with the airline flying between its Newcastle base, Aberdeen, Belfast City and Manchester. A period of consolidation then followed, until in 1995 a programme of expansion began with a £7 million investment by New Aviation Holdings which now wholly owns the company. With the expansion of both services and equipment, another name change resulted in the adoption of Gill Airways, a title considered more suited to the carrier's growing involvement in scheduled operations.

In addition to its own regional flights, it also operates services on behalf of KLM uk. These include the Newcastle-Stansted link which is

Opposite page:
G-BWDB — Aérospatiale ATR-72-202 of Gill Airways.

Right:
G-RMCT — Short SD3-60 Variant 100 of Gill Airways.

flown three-times daily with an ATR-42, plus four daily visits to Paris (CDG) from Stansted using an ATR-72. Similarly, the two airlines are associated with the Belfast-Prestwick and the Stansted-Hamburg sectors. In late 1997 Gill was contracted by Air France to operate the Newcastle-Paris services on its behalf, which resulted in one of the ATR-42s appearing in the French carrier's full livery. Gill Airways is still very involved in the nightly movement of mail with the help of the ATRs and SD3-60s.

FLEET:

Regn	Series	C/n
Aérospatiale ATR-42		
G-BVJP	300	371
G-ORFH	300	346
G-BXBV	310	245
G-WFEP	310	149
Aérospatiale ATR-72		
G-BWDA	202	444
G-BWDB	202	449
Short SD3-30		
G-BHHU	100	SH3042
Short SD3-60		
G-BLZT	100	SH3676
G-BVMX	300	SH3751
G-DASI	100	SH3606
G-OLAH	100	SH3604
G-RMCT	200	SH3656

Go

Head office: Enterprise House, Stansted Airport, Essex CM24 1QW
Tel: n/a   Fax: n/a

When British Airways released the news in late 1997 that it intended to create a low-cost subsidiary airline, it was identified only as Operation Blue Sky. A little more information about the future Stansted-based carrier was issued on 30 January 1998 when it was revealed that the chosen title was Go, a rather strange name but one that is certainly low-cost in paint. The airline declined to give any further details at that point other than to confirm that start-up would be in May. In order to achieve this target the airline had the difficult task of locating available Boeing 737-300s, the type selected for the fleet. A number of examples were located with Philippine Airlines but they were not due to be returned to the lessor until 2000. However, the airline agreed to an early termination of the lease with deliveries to Go expected between May and October 1998.

FLEET:

Regn	Series	C/n
G-	3Y0	24464
G-	3Y0	24465
G-	3Y0	24546
G-	3Y0	24547
G-	3Y0	24677
G-	3Y0	24678
G-	3Y0	24680
G-	3Y0	24681

HeavyLift Cargo Airlines
(NP/HLA)
Head Office: Stansted Airport, Stansted, Essex
CM24 1QW
Tel: (01279) 680611   Fax: (01279) 680615

When TAC HeavyLift began operations from Stansted in March 1980 it was at a time when freight airlines had been particularly hard hit by the world recession. Several had already ceased trading including Trans Meridian Air Cargo with which the newcomer had lingering ties. The choice of the Short Belfast was unusual especially since the well-proven CL-44 and Hercules were readily available. A considerable sum had been spent by the company in modifying the former RAF aircraft to the satisfaction of the CAA, the work consuming 20,000 man hours for design, another 25,000hr in engineering plus 120hr on flight trials. After the first restricted C of A in March 1980, the Belfast was finally awarded a full transport certificate on 23 March 1982, a piece of paper which in effect had cost over £3 million.

In common with the CL-44 and Hercules, the Belfast is able to lift heavy loads, but the internal dimensions produce a much longer hold with a definite advantage. Bulkier consignments can be handled, which was essentially the reason for the airline's entry into the air cargo business. Ironically it made the name HeavyLift something of a misnomer because many of the outsized loads carried are relatively light. Success for the company was not immediate since it took time to become known, but gradually customers were found, especially from within the aerospace industry. The movement of helicopters around the world became a regular source of employment, while the Dutch manufacturer Fokker discovered the usefulness of the Belfast to bring bent F-27s and F-28s back to the Netherlands for repair.

After the launch in 1980, the airline slowly expanded by introducing another two Belfasts into service, with a similar number stored at Southend for possible future use. In addition, HeavyLift operated the one-off Conroy converted CL-44-0, which although slightly smaller, was ideal for more general cargo work. During the first half of the 1990s the Stansted-based company also had a Boeing 707 on strength for similar employment, but eventually the type left the fleet. In the meantime there had been a major development with the setting up of a joint venture by HeavyLift and the Ukrainian company VolgaDnepr. As a result of this co-operation seven examples of the mighty Antonov An-124 freighters are available for world-wide cargo operations, two normally being based at the UK airport. With a payload of 120 tonnes, the aircraft are constantly in use. HeavyLift also has access to a pair of Ilyushin IL-76s, another useful large-capacity type.

During 1997 the first freighter conversions of the Airbus A300 passenger airliner were completed. Rapidly growing in popularity, a number of airlines have already ordered the type, HeavyLift being amongst them. The first of two was delivered in October 1997, but in the following month the machine took up Irish marks since it is leased from TransAer. Subsequently the A300 entered service by taking over the Amsterdam-Stockholm run under contract to KLM Cargo, while at other times it also maintained the regular cargo service between the Dutch airport and Bologna, Italy and Zaragoza in Spain. The second example was due for delivery in February 1998.

FLEET:

Regn	Series	C/n
Airbus A300B4		
EI-TLN	203F	047
G-HLAB	203F	045
Antonov An-124		
RA-82042	100	9773054055093
RA-82043	100	9773054155101
RA-82044	100	9773054155109
RA-82045	100	9773052255113
RA-82046	100	9773052255117
RA-82047	100	9773053259121
RA-82078	100	9773054559153
Ilyushin IL-76		
RA-76401	TD	1023412399
RA-76842	TD	-
Short SC5 Belfast		
G-BEPS	-	SH1822
G-HLFT	-	SH1819

Left:
RA-76401 — Ilyushin IL-76TD of HeavyLift Cargo Airlines.

Left:
G-BEPS — Short SC5 Belfast of HeavyLift Cargo Airlines.

Left:
RA-82042 — Antonov An-124 of HeavyLift/Volga Dnepr.

Hunting Cargo Airlines
(AG/ABR)
Head Office: East Midlands Airport, Castle Donington, Derbyshire DE74 2SA
Tel: (01332) 810081   Fax: (01332) 811419

The collapse of the freight airline Sagittair in September 1972 had its effect upon East Midlands-based Field Aircraft Services, the company hitherto responsible for the maintenance of the Armstrong-Whitworth Argosy fleet. These aircraft had been used for a number of contracts including the transportation of flowers and tomatoes from Guernsey to the UK mainland. In view of the sudden ending of its work, Fields decided to form a new airline to carry on with the operations, which led to the launch of Air Bridge Carriers. Warehouse facilities were obtained at the airport, while the necessary licences were obtained from the authorities to provide regular links with the Channel Islands. Three Argosies were employed for the work, although a Viscount was added to the fleet in 1974 for cargo and passenger charters. This particular example had been modified by Aer Lingus some years earlier and was one of the few to possess a large freight door in the forward fuselage. It was leased to Dan-Air for the latter's coach-air service between Lydd and Beauvais in 1975, but these duties lasted only one season.

During the second half of the 1970s British Airways began to retire its Vanguard/ Merchantman freighters, one of which was sold to Air Bridge in 1976. At this time the company had four Argosies and the Viscount in service, but thought had already been given to a suitable replacement. In the event, the Merchantman continued to be operated by BA until 1979 when the remaining five were also sold to the East Midlands company to join the single example already on strength. Thereafter the type was used extensively for freight charters to Europe and the Middle East, although it was the mid-1980s before the final Argosy sortie was flown in the colours of Elan Air.

By 1990 Air Bridge was considering its long-term requirements, eventually opting for the Lockheed Electra. The first example arrived during the year to be duly followed by more of the species before the company announced a change of name to Hunting Cargo Airlines in September 1992. A smart new livery was applied to the aircraft which continued Hunting's involvement in scheduled cargo services throughout Europe. Subsequently the airline began to add Boeing 727 freighters to its fleet in 1994, although it was not until October 1996 that the last ever flight was made by a Merchantman when G-APEP went into retirement at the Brooklands Museum at Weybridge, the scene of its first flight in 1961.

Currently Hunting Cargo is one of the major cargo carriers in Europe with an expanding overnight parcels network flown for DHL. Such is the volume of this business that a newly delivered Airbus A300B4 freighter is now gainfully employed with its maximum payload of 45 tonnes. In addition to this contract work, extensive freight services link numerous European cities. During 1997 Hunting decided to consolidate all of the airline's activities in Ireland, which also brought the closing down of the UK operation. This decision resulted in all of the aircraft that still carried British registrations being allocated Irish identities to serve with Hunting Cargo Airlines (Ireland) Ltd. On the other hand the B727s that had been flown on behalf of TNT for several years received Danish registrations, but this followed the loss of the contract to Sterling European.

FLEET:

Regn	Series	C/n
Boeing 727		
EI-HCA	225F	20382
EI-HCB	223F	19492
EI-HCC	223F	19480
EI-HCD	223F	20185
EI-HCI	223F	20183
EI-LCH	282F	20466
Lockheed L188 Electra		
EI-CET	CF	1144
EI-CHF	CF	1129
EI-CHX	CF	2006
EI-CHZ	CF	2015
Airbus A300B4		
E1-EAT	203F	116

Isles of Scilly Skybus (5Y/IOS)

Head Office: Land's End Aerodrome, St Just,
Penzance, Cornwall TR19 7RL
Tel: (01736) 787017   Fax: (01736) 788366

Although only a relatively short distance from the mainland, the sea journey to the Scilly Isles can be something of an endurance test. The advent of air travel brought hope of an alternative, but it was 1935 before proving flights were operated using land between Sennen and St Just as the Cornish terminal. Not surprisingly, the venture proved a success resulting in the opening of Land's End Airport in September 1937. Services were initially operated by Channel Air Ferries which later became a part of Great Western & Southern Airlines.

Several new routes were introduced by the company, but at the outbreak of war it was the Scilly route that continued in view of its strategic importance. Regular sorties were flown until 3 June 1941 when the airline lost Dragon G-ACPY, believed to have been the victim of the Luftwaffe. After a short period of suspension, operations restarted in October with three return flights each day. The link was thereafter maintained at this frequency until increased to six in 1945. Subsequently British European Airways became responsible for the link, for some years employing the last of its Rapide fleet until the introduction of helicopter equipment.

Although the regular services became very popular with the added convenience of a Penzance heliport, in 1984 the Isles of Scilly Steamship Company decided to provide some competition using Britten-Norman Islanders. Unfortunately a delay in receiving the necessary approval from the CAA meant that the first services were not flown until 6 April 1987. Known as the Isles of Scilly Skybus, the airline began with six daily return trips, but gradually the demand warranted a considerable increase to this figure. Through the succeeding years up to 40 rotations per day have been operated in the peak season, with the schedules continuing at a reduced level during the winter months.

For almost 10 years the airline relied upon the reliable Islanders for all of the passenger and freight services, but in 1994 the fleet was reduced to three although at the same time a DHC-6 Twin Otter was acquired by the company. The larger capacity type was then employed on several new routes that provided access to the Scillies from Bristol, Exeter, Newquay, Plymouth and Southampton several times per week in the summer season. In fact, the aircraft involved was not a stranger to the area since it had at one time been operated on a similar network by Brymon Airways.

Fleet:

Regn	Series	C/n
BN-2A Islander		
G-SBUS	-	3013
BN-2B Islander		
G-BUBN	-	2270
G-SSKY	-	2247
DHC-6 Twin Otter		
G-BIHO	310	738

Jersey European Airways (JY/JEA)

Head Office: Terminal Building, Exeter Airport,
Exeter, Devon EX5 2BD
Tel: (01392) 366669   Fax: (01392) 366151

On 1 January 1969 a group of former British United (Channel Islands) pilots founded Intra Airways in order to provide scheduled air services between Jersey, Guernsey and Alderney with a DC-3. However, before operations started on 14 March, it was realised that Aurigny Air Services was already providing efficient inter-island links with Islanders, so the company turned its attention to passenger and freight charter work.

Regular sorties to points in northern France were well supported by Jersey holidaymakers, for whom a day return was long enough to satisfy the curiosity. Similarly, Intra flew services from a number of UK airports to Jersey during the summer seasons in the 1970s, eventually possessing a six-strong fleet of DC-3s and two Islanders. The latter were used for new routes to such places as Deauville and Le Touquet, but since the ventures were not particularly successful both aircraft had been sold by late 1975.

Towards the end of the decade the airline acquired a trio of Viscounts from British

Midland, but in November 1979 a new company was established at Jersey to take over the affairs of both Intra Airways and the Bournemouth-based Express Air Services. Known as Jersey European Airways, the carrier immediately inherited a large network of scheduled passenger and freight services involving a considerable number of airports in the UK and mainland Europe. In due course the fleet was reduced in size and variety, Islanders, Bandeirantes and Twin Otters being employed for many of the services, until the advent of the Short SD3-30 and SD3-60 in the mid-1980s.

By this time the two founding companies had reverted to their original independent status, but in 1983 JEA was purchased by Jack Walker's Walkersteel Group of Blackburn (later the Walker Aviation Group), already the owner of Spacegrand Aviation based at Blackpool. Similar in size to its new associate, the latter began operating scheduled services across the Irish Sea in August 1981. It was inevitable that the two airlines would be merged at some point, an event that took place on 26 October 1985 when the name Jersey European was adopted and operations transferred to Exeter.

In the light of continuous expansion, two 52-seat Friendship 500s were added to the fleet in 1988, but although the airline's policy was to re-equip totally with this type, it was found very difficult to locate any available examples. As an interim measure it was decided to lease three HS748s, the first entering service on the Blackpool routes while the second pair were based in the south. These mainly replaced the SD3-60s, although one of the latter was retained for the Exeter-Manchester link which released the sole Bandeirante still in the fleet. In late 1990 JEA managed to acquire six Friendship 500s from the Australian operator East West Airlines which, after overhaul and refurbishment, were ready for the coming summer programme.

Already one of the leading regional carriers in the UK, in 1993 JEA announced that it was leasing two BAe 146-200s and one Series 300 from the manufacturer for use on the airline's busy Belfast City-Gatwick and the Gatwick-Channel Islands routes. A minimum of four flights per day were planned initially with the 146s, although others would be operated by Friendships. The introduction of the jets, together with the key network expansion, elevated JEA to the forefront of the domestic UK airlines, competing directly against British Airways and British Midland. Subsequently the airline has increased its 146 fleet considerably to cope with the service frequency increases and the introduction of new sectors. In terms of aircraft movements, JEA is now the largest carrier operating from Northern Ireland and the second largest scheduled airline at Birmingham which is playing an increasingly important role as a hub. Domestic and international destinations now served by JEA include Belfast City and International, Birmingham, Blackpool, Bristol, Derry, Exeter, Gatwick, Glasgow, Guernsey, Heathrow, Isle of Man, Jersey, Leeds/Bradford, Paris and Stansted.

London's third airport has also received increased attention with six daily flights to Belfast, a far cry from the solitary Saturday visit by a Jersey-bound Twin Otter in the early 1980s. It seems possible that more routes will be added to overcome the slot shortage at Gatwick, the alternative being the introduction of larger capacity types such as the A320 or 737, although neither could economically use Guernsey. In addition to its own impressive coverage, JEA became a franchise operator for Air France Express in 1997. This involved flying the latter's schedules between Heathrow, Lyon and Toulouse with a pair of 146s painted in the French carrier's livery. For the future, while there are no immediate plans to retire the turboprops, JEA is nevertheless evaluating the 50-seat regional jet market.

Left:
G-JEAM — BAe 146-300 of Jersey European Airways.

FLEET:

Regn	Series	C/n
BAe 146		
G-JEAJ	200	E2099
G-JEAK	200	E2103
G-JEAL	300	E3129
G-JEAM	300	E3128
G-JEAO	100	E1010
G-JEAR	200	E2018
G-JEAS	200	E2020
G-JEAT	100	E1071
G-JEAU	100	E1035
G-JEAV	200	E2064
G-JEAW	200	E2059
G-JEAX	200	E2136
Fokker F-27 Friendship		
G-JEAD	500	10627
G-JEAE	500	10633
G-JEAF	500	10637
G-JEAG	500	10639
G-JEAH	500	10669
G-JEAI	500	10672
Short SD3-60		
G-OBHD	200	SH3714
G-OBLK	200	SH3712

Right:
G-JEAH — Fokker F-27-500 of Jersey European Airways.

Right:
G-OBLK — Short SD3-60 Variant 100 of Jersey European Airways.

Right:
G-AVMK — BAC One-Eleven 510ED operated by Jersey European until March 1998.

KLM uk

Head Office: Stansted Airport, Stansted, Essex CM24 1AE
Tel: (01279) 660400   Fax: (01279) 660330

In October 1979 it was announced that British Island Airways and Air Anglia were to merge at the beginning of the New Year. Both carriers had originally been formed 10 years or so earlier, both as a result of mergers. In the case of BIA its antecedents could be traced back to the early postwar years when Silver City, Manx and Jersey Airlines were operational. Eventually becoming a member of British United, it was not included in the sale of its parent to Caledonian, remaining instead a part of the British & Commonwealth Group. As British Island Airways it operated a large network of routes with an all-Herald fleet, although it had also entered the IT charter business with three One-Elevens just prior to the merger with Air Anglia.

The latter had been formed in July 1970 by the amalgamation of three small charter carriers: Norfolk Airways, Anglian Air Charter and Rig Air. From the start its scheduled services were aimed particularly at the eastern side of Britain by including all the major airports in its coverage. After a careful start with DC-3s, modernisation began in 1972 with the arrival of the first Fokker Friendship. Air Anglia remained the only UK company to operate the type into the 1980s, by which time it had also become a member of the British & Commonwealth Group. Prior to the merger with BIA, considerable thought had been given to which jet type should be selected to supersede the Friendship on some routes. Although an admirable aircraft which had proved reliable and economic on the longer sectors such as Edinburgh-Paris, there was a distinct danger of losing passengers to the faster One-Elevens of British Airways. Finally Air Anglia decided on the F-28 Fellowship, two of which were ordered for delivery in mid-1979.

On 16 January 1980 the combined BIA and Air Anglia became Air UK, which was immediately elevated into the position of the country's third largest scheduled operator after BA and British Caledonian. Some form of standardisation was necessary which quickly led to the departure of the new F-28s on lease, leaving the One-Elevens dedicated to IT work. During the first summer season, the scheduled route network included 33 airports in the UK and on the Continent, with most of the aircraft remaining at their normal bases. Nevertheless a degree of flexibility was now possible by slotting Friendships into Herald rotas when necessary. Plans were also made for the gradual withdrawal of the latter aircraft, but in fact it was not until 28 June 1985 that G-APWJ operated the type's final schedule for the airline.

The early 1980s brought a good deal of reorganisation by the company, including some significant cutbacks in services while some airports were dropped completely. One of the casualties was Stansted which had earlier been earmarked by Air Anglia for steady expansion. The absence proved to be only temporary because on 2 November 1981 a Friendship, appropriately registered G-STAN, flew the inaugural twice-daily service from Stansted to Amsterdam, the airport's first international schedule for 10 years. By this time Air UK Commuter had been formed using the smaller capacity Bandeirante, Short SD3-30 and SD3-60 on some routes, the last of the

Right:
G-BTTP — BAe 146-300 of Air UK. To become KLM uk.

Above:
G-UKTC — Fokker 50 of Air UK. To become KLM uk.

latter species remaining with the company into the 1990s.

There was an event of importance on 14 December 1987 when a BAe 146 began work on the airline's Heathrow-Guernsey link, while a second example was ordered for use on the Aberdeen and Edinburgh-Amsterdam schedules. The type quickly became popular with passengers and was the mainstay of Air UK's operations in the early 1990s until joined by the Fokker 100 in 1992 as a further step in the modernisation programme. Together, the types have since been responsible for the impressive growth in the services provided by Air UK. A start was made on the retirement of the faithful Friendships in 1994, with Fokker 50s taking over the duties in most cases. However, a few of the older breed continued on the Channel Islands services until the arrival of ATR-72s in the spring of 1998 for operations under the marketing name of Air UK Channel Hopper.

For many years Air UK has been associated with KLM, the Dutch national carrier, eventually leading to the latter taking a 45% share in the British company in 1995. In a further move, the marketing departments of the two organisations were integrated on 1 April 1997, followed three months later by the announcement that Air UK was to become a wholly-owned subsidiary of KLM. There had been indications of change for some time, particularly with the number of routes dropped in favour of direct flights to Amsterdam and its vast network of worldwide destinations. There was confirmation that Air UK was to be

Left:
G-UKFO — Fokker 100 of KLM uk.
KLM uk

73

rebranded, but it was 30 January 1998 before there was a formal launch. From that date the trading name of the British company became KLM uk in order to reflect its ties with its Dutch parent, the same prefix also being applied to the Channel Hopper division. It was planned to repaint five aircraft by the end of February, with half the fleet completed by June.

FLEET:

Regn	Series	C/n
Aérospatiale ATR-72		
G-UKTJ	202	509
G-UKTK	202	519
G-UKTL	202	523
G-UKTM	202	508
G-UKTN	202	496
BAe 146		
G-BSNR	300	E3165
G-BSNS	300	E3169
G-BTTP	300	E3203
G-BUHC	300	E3193
G-UKAC	300	E3142
G-UKAG	300	E3162
G-UKHP	300	E3123
G-UKID	300	E3157
G-UKJF	100	E1011
G-UKRC	300	E3158
G-UKSC	300	E3125
Fokker 50		
G-UKTA	-	20246
G-UKTB	-	20247
G-UKTC	-	20249
G-UKTD	-	20256
G-UKTE	-	20270
G-UKTF	-	20271
G-UKTG	-	20276
G-UKTH	-	20277
G-UKTI	-	20279
Fokker 100		
G-UKFA	-	11246
G-UKFB	-	11247
G-UKFC	-	11263
G-UKFD	-	11259
G-UKFE	-	11260
G-UKFF	-	11274
G-UKFG	-	11275
G-UKFH	-	11277
G-UKFI	-	11279
G-UKFJ	-	11248
G-UKFK	-	11249
G-UKFL	-	11268
G-UKFM	-	11269
G-UKFN	-	11270
G-UKFO	-	11271
G-UKFP	-	11272
G-UKFR	-	11273

Leisure International Airways (LEI/ULE)

Head Office: Leisure House, Church Road, Lowfield Heath, Crawley, Sussex RH11 0PQ
Tel: (01293) 843321   Fax: (01293) 843320

The airline was formed jointly by Air UK and the tour operator Unijet in June 1987 for the purpose of flying European IT charters. Operations began from Stansted with a pair of leased Boeing 737-200s on 30 April 1988, but these were replaced in October by the first of the ordered 172-seat Series 400s. In due course the fleet size increased as did the number of UK airports served, until in February 1992 Leisure International was formed as a subsidiary company. Equipped with a pair of Boeing 767-300ERs, the airline began flying transatlantic charters to Florida and the Caribbean area in April 1993, the aircraft achieving some impressive utilisation figures.

During 1996 Unijet gained complete control of Air UK Leisure whereupon the name was dropped and a re-equipment programme announced. Three Airbus A320s were acquired to replace the 737s which were eventually transferred to KLM. In the longer term Leisure opted for the Airbus A321, the first example being delivered on 7 May 1997. It had been planned originally that from then on the airline would receive one aircraft per year until five were on strength, but in the event deliveries were accelerated. As the number of A321s in service increases, so the smaller A320s will be returned to the lessor.

The final break with Air UK came in early 1997 when Leisure moved its headquarters to Gatwick, although its A320s still operate services from Stansted for Unijet and other tour operators such as Sunworld. Towards the end of the year Leisure announced that it had ordered two Pratt & Whitney PW4168A-powered A330-200s for delivery during the first quarter of 2000. These are intended to replace the two Boeing 767-300ERs on the transatlantic charter duties, the 380-seat capacity and 5,280 miles range being useful features to handle the anticipated growth of the long-haul market.

Above:
G-UKLK — Airbus A320-212 of Leisure International Airways.

Below:
G-UKLI — Boeing 767-39HER of Leisure International Airways.

FLEET:

Regn	Series	C/n
Airbus A320		
G-UKLK	212	343
G-UKLL	212	189
Airbus A321		
G-UNID	211	677
G-UNIE	211	781
G-UNIF	211	-
G-UNIG	211	-
G-UNIH	211	-
Boeing 767		
G-UKLH	39HER	26256
G-UKLI	39HER	26257
Airbus A330		
G-UNIA	200	-
G-UNIB	200	-

Above:
G-UKLO — Airbus A321-211 of Leisure International Airways (now G-UNID).

Loganair (LC/LOG)

Head Office: St Andrews Drive, Glasgow Airport, Paisley, Renfrewshire PA3 2TG
Tel: (0141) 848 7594   Fax: (0141) 887 6020

Formed on 1 February 1962, this subsidiary of the Royal Bank of Scotland became the country's leading independent airline. A large network of scheduled services were introduced, many of them connecting the smaller islands off the north coast with the mainland. A fleet of Britten-Norman Islanders and Trislanders were employed, both ideal to cope with the rough airstrips. Later Twin Otters took over the busier sectors thereby providing additional capacity where needed, this type gradually replacing the Trislanders. In 1973 Loganair became responsible for the air ambulance service previously in the hands of BEA, an essential life-line for the inhabitants that depend upon this link. By the 1980s the airline had added several other types to its fleet including the Bandeirante and Short SD3-30, with both being used for the main links with Edinburgh and Glasgow.

In 1983 British Midland acquired Loganair, both companies becoming members of the Airlines of Britain Group in 1987. Thereafter the Scottish carrier began steadily to expand its activities to include services to Northern Ireland and England. A pair of Friendships were leased from the parent and the carrier applied to take over the licences previous held by British Caledonian for routes from Gatwick to Scotland. The growing coverage was also responsible for an order for two BAe 146s, the first of which was delivered in July 1988. The airline subsequently took delivery of a number of BAe ATPs and Jetstream 31s and 41s, all needed for the network as it relentlessly extended into southern England, the Channel Islands and mainland Europe.

However, the Group embarked on a major reorganisation scheme in early 1994 which resulted in Loganair transferring routes and aircraft to Manx. Most of the services retained were the internal Scottish sectors flown by Islanders and SD3-60s, some of the latter being former Manx machines. In July Loganair signed a franchise agreement with British Airways, whereupon the fleet was repainted in the flag carrier's livery. An unusual situation arose in October 1996 when the airline became associated with British Regional Airlines, but in the following February Loganair was restored to its original independent state by a management buy-out. It now once again concentrates its activities on the inter-island flights around the Scottish coast together with meeting the ambulance service requirements. These are carried out with Islanders and one Twin Otter, all painted in the controversial BA colours introduced in 1997.

FLEET:

Regn	Series	C/n
BN-2B Islander		
G-BJOP	26	2132
G-BLDV	26	2179
G-BLNJ	26	2189
G-BLNW	26	2197
G-BPCA	26	2198
DHC-6 Twin Otter		
G-BVVK	310	666

Love Air (4J/LOV)

Head Office: Building 44, Stansted Airport, Essex CM24 1QE
Tel: (01279) 680144   Fax: (01279) 680356

The airline operates daily scheduled services between Biggin Hill and Le Touquet in northern France using a fleet of nine-seat Navajo aircraft. In addition to this regular work, Love Air, which is a division of the London Flight Centre based at Stansted, flies passenger and cargo charters throughout Europe.

FLEET:

Regn	Series	C/n
Piper PA-31 Turbo Navajo		
G-BEZL	310	31-7712054
G-EEAC	310	31-761
Piper PA-31 Navajo Chieftain		
G-CAFZ	350	31-7405429
G-HVRD	350	31-7305052

Maersk Air Ltd (VB/MSK)

Head Office: Maersk Air House, 2245-49 Coventry Road, Birmingham B26 3NG
Tel: (0121) 743 9090   Fax: (0121) 743 4123

The airline can trace its history back to 1983 with the founding of Birmingham Executive Airways, which aimed to provide business class services on a number of routes at one time plied by British Airways. The inaugural flight was to Zürich and Copenhagen on 9 June, but it was November before further expansion brought Milan into the network, followed by Genoa in April 1984. The company was the first British airline to introduce the SAAB 340, but various problems with the aircraft finally forced its return to the manufacturer. A new type was therefore urgently needed which resulted in the choice of the Gulfstream 1.

A relaunch of the operator took place in October 1987, but in November 1988 the airline was acquired by The Plimsoll Line, the major shareholders being British Airways and Maersk Air, each with a 40% interest. Renamed Birmingham European Airways, the company quickly expanded its coverage and fleet which comprised three Jetstreams, three Gulfstreams, two Fokker 50s and five BAC One-Eleven 400s. There was a merger between Brymon Airways and Birmingham European in 1992, but this venture lasted only a year before being divided once again into its two original parts. BEA was bought by Maersk Air, while the Brymon element became a wholly-owned subsidiary of British Airways. The Birmingham-based airline was therefore now a member of the Danish A. P. Moller Group taking the name Maersk Air Ltd.

It was the first instance of a foreign company taking advantage of European Union legislation which allows 100% ownership of an airline in another EU country.

Initially Maersk employed the aircraft it had inherited, but a modernisation programme to replace the ageing One-Elevens was becoming urgent. The first steps were taken in 1996 when three Boeing 737-500s were leased from the Danish parent company. These released three of the One-Eleven 400s, while a Jetstream 41 was introduced on the Newcastle run to replace the smaller Series 31 machines. A fourth 737 was ordered for delivery in early 1998, but the carrier decided to order three Canadair RJ200s as replacements for the remaining One-Elevens, one (G-AWYV) being leased from European Aviation. Maersk has also taken options on a further 12 RJs which can be taken as either the 50-seat or 70-seat variant, but the decision will not be taken until after the newcomers are in service during the second quarter of 1998.

FLEET:

Regn	Series	C/n
BAC One-Eleven		
G-AWYR	501EX	174
	(until end of June 1998)	
G-AWYS	501EX	175
	(until end of July 1998)	
G-AWYV	501EX	178
BAe Jetstream		
G-MSKJ	4101	41034
Boeing 737		
G-MSKA	5L9	24859
G-MSKB	5L9	24928
G-MSKC	5L9	25066
G-MSKD	5L9	24778
Canadair RJ		
G-MSKK	200LR	7226
G-MSKL	200LR	7247
G-MSKM	200LR	–

Above:
G-MSKC — Boeing 737-5L9 of Maersk Air (UK)/BA. *AST Photography*

Manx Airlines (JE/MNX)

Head Office: Isle of Man (Ronaldsway) Airport, Ballasalla, Isle of Man IM9 2JE
Tel: (01624) 826000   Fax: (01624) 826001

The airline celebrated its 50th anniversary in 1997 since it was founded in 1947 as Manx Air Charters equipped with two Rapides. An association with a short-lived company known as Air Charter Services produced more of the type, thereby enabling the airline to fly its first scheduled service to Carlisle from 1950.

Further routes were established in due course, including a link between the island, Newcastle and Glasgow. This step was made possible by the introduction of a pair of 34-seat DC-3s in 1953, whereupon the company took the opportunity to change its name to Manx Airlines.

However, three years later in May 1956, it was taken over by the British Aviation Services Group to become the northern division of Silver City Airways. This resulted in the transfer of Bristol Wayfarers to the Ronaldsway-based carrier which thereafter employed them on its passenger services until one of the type crashed in February 1958. Finally, after 11 successful years of operations, the airline was fully integrated into Silver City and the Manx name disappeared.

This remained the case for the next 24 years or so, until on 1 November 1982, the present day Manx was created by British Midland and Air UK. The new company was launched with services to Heathrow and major regional airports, using a mixed fleet of aircraft that included an 18-seat Bandeirante, two Friendships and a 73-seat Viscount. A BAC One-Eleven eventually replaced the latter on the London route, which in turn was substituted by the leased BAe 146-100 G-OJET in 1987. In the meantime Short SD3-60s had been acquired and employed on the shorter routes plus the new Liverpool-Heathrow services taken over from British Midland. This sector soon became the responsibility of a SAAB 340, the only one of its kind on the UK register at the time, but the type left Manx after a couple of years or so.

For the remainder of the decade, the airline continued to expand its operations and fleet, ordering three new BAe ATP turboprops in July 1988 and introducing the first example during the next year. In a breakaway from its island home, the major development of a Cardiff hub was announced in October 1990, the Dublin service becoming a part of a network linking Brussels, Paris, Belfast and Glasgow using ATP and Jetstream 31 aircraft. The Channel Islands were later added, while the Belfast sorties were extended to Aberdeen.

In the same year two new companies were created known as Manx Airlines (Holdings) Ltd and the subsidiary Manx Airlines (Europe) Ltd. This step was necessary because the Isle of Man is not part of the European Community, therefore Manx did not have automatic access

Above:
G-MIMA — BAe 146-200 of Manx Airlines.

to UK domestic and inter-European routes. In reality Manx Airlines and Manx Airlines (Europe) continued to operate as a single carrier until January 1995, when the latter became a British Airways franchise with its aircraft carrying the flag carrier's livery and titles. It became responsible for all routes with the exception of those radiating from the Isle of Man which remained with Manx Airlines.

Subsequently Manx Airlines (Europe) became British Regional Airlines in September 1996, while Loganair's main routes were taken over, helping the holding company to become the UK's leading regional carrier. Unlike the various mergers and amalgamations in the 1950s which caused the Manx name to disappear, services to and from Ronaldsway are still maintained by island-based aircraft which carry the red and green livery with titles that continue the airline's affinity with the Manx Gaelic language. Points served from the island on a year-round basis are Birmingham, Cardiff, Glasgow, Heathrow, Jersey, Leeds/Bradford, Liverpool, Luton, Manchester and Southampton. Seasonal routes link Newcastle with the Isle of Man, while flights are operated between Cardiff and Dublin and from Jersey to both Cork and the Irish capital.

FLEET:

Regn	Series	C/n
BAe ATP		
G-MANA	-	2056
G-MANB	-	2055
G-MANC	-	2054
G-MANO	-	2006
G-MANU	-	2008
BAe Jetstream		
G-MAJA	41	41032
BAe 146		
G-MIMA	200	E2079

Left:
G-MANA — BAe ATP of Manx Airlines.

Right:
G-MAJA — BAe Jetstream 41 of Manx Airlines.

Monarch Airlines (ZB/MON)
Head Office: Luton International Airport,
Bedfordshire LU2 9NU
Tel: (01582) 400000 Fax: (01582) 411000

On 1 June 1967 the Cosmos Tour Group formed its own airline to operate its charter services. Known as Monarch Airlines, the company began its revenue-earning activities on 5 April 1968 when one of its two Britannias flew a load of IT passengers from Luton to Madrid. Throughout the summer months the airline visited numerous destinations in the Mediterranean area with a fleet that had grown substantially due to the unfortunate demise of British Eagle. By the early 1970s nine of the popular Britannias were on strength, but inevitably the need for progress meant that it was necessary to move into jet operations. Monarch therefore began to evaluate suitable types, eventually deciding to acquire some former Northwest Airlines Boeing 720s. The first was handed over on 15 September 1971, giving the airline the distinction of becoming the first UK operator of the type.

The collapse of Court Line presented the opportunity for more business, so three One-Elevens were leased in 1975 for use at some of the smaller airports. Nevertheless it was January 1976 before the airline's final Britannia was withdrawn from use, leaving Monarch to operate the IT charters with its B720s and One-Elevens. In the early 1980s the first steps were taken towards acquiring modern equipment when the first of a number of B737s was delivered, but more significantly Monarch became the first independent to put the Boeing 757 into service in March 1983. The type has subsequently remained with the company, but the latter has recently shown a preference for various Airbus products.

Elsewhere, Monarch played an important part in the founding of EuroBerlin by supplying and operating six B737-300s. These were employed on German domestic routes at a time when Lufthansa was not allowed to fly into the nation's former capital.

Nowadays Monarch operates IT charters for many of the leading tour operators from airports such as Birmingham, Gatwick, Glasgow, Leeds/Bradford, Luton, Manchester and Stansted. While the majority serve the European holiday areas, long-haul sorties are undertaken across the Atlantic, to Africa and the Far East. In addition to this charter work, the airline also offers a number of scheduled services which link Luton with Alicante, Gibraltar, Malaga, Menorca, Palma de Mallorca and Tenerife.

Orders have been placed for A321s and A330s, with once again Monarch becoming the first UK carrier to order the species. Both types are due for delivery in time for the 1999 summer season, but in the meantime the airline has leased a second DC-10-30 for its long-haul commitments in 1998.

FLEET:

Regn	Series	C/n
Airbus A300		
G-MAJS	605R	604
G-MONR	605R	540
G-MONS	605R	556
G-OJMR	605R	605
Airbus A320		
G-MONW	212	391
G-MONX	212	392
G-MONY	212	279
G-MONZ	212	446
G-MPCD	212	379
G-OZBA	212	422
G-OZBB	212	389
Airbus A321		
G-OZBC	232	633
G-	232	-
G-	232	-
Airbus A330		
G-	200	-
G-	200	-
Boeing 757		
DAJB	2T7	23770
MONB	2T7	22780
MOND	2T7	22960
MONE	2T7	23293
MONJ	2T7	24104
MONK	2T7	24105
Douglas DC-10		
G-DMCA	30	48266
OO-LRM	30	46998
	(summer lease 1998)	
Lockheed L1011 TriStar		
TF-ABU	1	1052
	(standby aircraft until November 1998)	

Left:
G-MONS — Airbus A300-605R of Monarch Airlines.

Right:
G-DMCA — Douglas DC-10-30 of Monarch Airlines.

Left:
G-MONW — Airbus A320-212 of Monarch Airlines.

Right:
G-MONJ — Boeing 757-2T7 of Monarch Airlines.

Peach Air (KGC)

Head Office: c/o Caledonian Airways Ltd,
Caledonian House, Gatwick Airport, Crawley,
West Sussex RH6 0LF
Tel: (01293) 668280   Fax: (01293) 668353

After several seasons of over capacity, the tour operators trimmed the number of charter flights available in the mid-1990s, but by 1997 this had changed to a shortage of seats. In addition, the industry had not displayed a very good image to the public in recent years with instances of poor time-keeping and unreliability, leading to frequent expressions of general dissatisfaction from travellers. In an attempt to prevent such situations Caledonian Airways and the tour operator Goldcrest jointly founded Peach Air as a low-cost subsidiary in 1996. Operations began from both Manchester and Gatwick for the 1997 summer season by flying IT charters for the Inspirations Group to resorts around the Mediterranean area. Peach Air has no aircraft of its own, but uses equipment wet-leased from Sabre Airways and Air Atlanta Iceland. The latter supplies TriStars usually in an all-white scheme but with the addition of a large Peach logo on the fin.

FLEET:

Regn	Series	C/n
Boeing 737		
G-SBEA	204ADV	21694
G-SBEB	204ADV	20807
Lockheed L1011 TriStar		
TF-ABE	1	1022
TF-ABH	1	1054
TF-ABM	50	1072
TF-ABT	100	1231

Sabre Airways (TJ/SBE)

Head Office: 12 The Merlin Centre, County
Oak Way, Crawley, West Sussex RH11 7XA
Tel: (01293) 410727   Fax: (01293) 410737

The airline was founded in 1994, with operations starting on 17 December. For the first 12 months it flew under Air Foyle's Operator's Certificate, but Sabre was awarded its own licence on 13 December 1995. The initial equipment comprised a pair of Boeing 737-200s which were employed mainly for IT charter work on behalf of Goldcrest. Previously this seat broker had contracted much of its business to the now defunct Ambassador Airways, which in fact had used the same two aircraft. In 1995 Sabre added a pair of former Dan-Air Boeing 727s to its fleet, one of which has since been upgraded with a FedEx hush-kit to comply with the Stage 3 noise regulations. This modification allows night operations at Gatwick and Manchester without penalty. During 1997 the two 737s were wet-leased or sub-leased to Peach Air, an associated carrier of Sabre, while the latter announced its intention to introduce two of the new generation 189-seat 737-800s, both to be leased from ILFC before the start of the 1998 summer programme. These will undertake services from Birmingham, Gatwick, Luton, Manchester and Newcastle to destinations around the Mediterranean and the Canary Islands.

Right:
G-BNNI — Boeing 727-276 of Sabre Airways.

FLEET:

Regn	Series	C/n
Boeing 737		
G-SBEA	204ADV	21694
G-SBEB	204ADV	20807
G-	8Q8	28226
G-	8Q8	28218
Boeing 727		
G-BNNI	276	20950
G-BPND	2D3	21021

Sky-Trek Airlines

Head Office: Lydd Airport, Lydd, Kent TN29 9QI
Tel: (01797) 320000   Fax: (01797) 321055

A subsidiary of Atlantic Bridge Aviation, the owner of Lydd Airport, Sky-Trek began twice-daily services between its base and Le Touquet in 1997. This route was relentlessly flown by Silver City's Bristol Freighters in the 1950s, but such times have sadly long gone.

Nevertheless, despite the availability of the Channel Tunnel and the much improved sea ferries, there remains sufficient interest in the aerial crossing to make the venture worthwhile. Sky-Trek envisages the service being used mainly for day excursions by holidaymakers in the vicinity of Lydd. The attractions of the French town are sufficient to justify the £60 return fare for the journey that the Trislanders can complete in 20min. The carrier's parent company has already completely refurbished the terminal at Lydd which has been very much underused since the end of the car ferry era more than 25 years ago. It is hoped to encourage other carriers to the airport which has plans to extend the existing runway to 5,900ft (1,800m), thereby enabling jet types to use the facilities. In the meantime Sky-Trek hopes to introduce other cross-Channel routes to France, the Netherlands and the Channel Islands.

FLEET:

Regn	Series	C/n
BN-2A Trislander		
G-BDOT	III-2	1025
G-BEDP	III-2	1039

South Coast Airways (GAD)

Head Office: 73 Gladstone Road, Boscombe, Bournemouth, Dorset BH7 6HD
Tel: (01202) 304855   Fax: (01202) 304855

The airline was founded to satisfy the demand for special flights in the ever-popular DC-3. In addition to local pleasure sorties, trips are arranged to various air show events from a number of departure points during the season. Based at Bournemouth, the DC-3 entered the UK register in July 1994 after a period in France as F-GEOM. Delivered in 1943, the machine subsequently was operated postwar by CSA Czech Airlines, later reverting to military use with the French Navy. Now equipped with 32 seats, the immaculate South Coast Airways DC-3 gives much pleasure to its many passengers.

FLEET:

Regn	Series	C/n
Douglas DC-3		
G-DAKK	C-47A	9798

Right:
G-DAKK — Douglas DC-3 of South Coast Airways. International Airways.

Streamline Aviation (SSW)

Head Office: Office 12, Exeter Airport, Exeter, Devon EX5 2BD
Tel: (01392) 361795   Fax: (01392) 360424

Although based at Exeter, many of the company's activities are carried out at a number of UK airports. Nightly freight operations link Southend, Luton and East Midlands with European destinations such as Amsterdam, Brussels and Dublin. In addition to the contract work, ad hoc charters are also undertaken. Streamline expanded during 1996 following the takeover of Southend-based Willowair.

FLEET:

Regn	Series	C/n
BN-2A Mk.III-2 Trislander		
G-OJAV	-	1024
Embraer EMB-110 Bandeirante		
G-OCSI	P2	270
G-OCSZ	P1	369
G-OHIG	P1	235
Short SD3-30		
G-BITW	100	SH3070
G-LEDN	100	SH3064
G-IOCS	100	SH3057

Suckling Airways (CB/SAY)

Head Office: Cambridge Airport, Newmarket Road, Cambridge CB5 8RT
Tel: (01223) 292525   Fax: (01223) 292160

When it was announced that a new airline proposed to start scheduled services from the grass airfield at Ipswich, the prospects for success did not appear particularly encouraging. Many years had passed since the airport handled its final Channel Airways' flight in 1972, leaving the terminal building to deteriorate gently, with peeling paint bearing witness to the lack of activity. Suddenly this changed when in April 1986 work was feverishly carried out to restore an air of well-being, before the start of a new chapter in the site's history, it was hoped.

On 23 April Suckling Airways ceased to be a paper airline when it took delivery of its first machine, a Dornier Do228, the order becoming the 100th received by the manufacturer and the first of the type for the UK register. It was the culmination of many months of planning during which time the company gained the licences for the Ipswich-Amsterdam and Rotterdam routes. These were

Above:
G-BWWT — Dornier Do328-110 of Suckling Airways.

Above:
GBWIR — Dornier Do328 of Suckling Airways.

originally intended to be flown on a triangular pattern by a leased Twin Otter, but before this became a reality, another factor brought a slight change to the proposed operation. Already aware that the market existed for a link between Manchester and Ipswich, a licence was sought and received to provide schedules linking these two points. Timings permitted a through service to Amsterdam, therefore qualifying the carrier for one of the welcome grants from British Airways. With this development, the Twin Otter was no longer considered suitable, so in an unusual move by a brand-new airline, Suckling decided to buy its aircraft rather than lease.

Although aiming for an inaugural flight on 21 April, late delivery forced a postponement; the cause resting with a delay with the British-

Above:
G-BMMR — Dornier Do228-200 of Suckling Airways.

made covers for the 18 seats. It also meant that the two flight crews on strength had no time for training or route-proving sorties, while the CAA still had to stamp its final seal of approval on the venture. Four cabin staff were recruited by the airline, two of whom carried out the flying duties while the second pair handled the ground-based reception, check-in and general administration. The quartet regularly rotated their activities so that they were familiar with every aspect of the organisation. It was no accident that all were quite short, a useful feature when walking along the 228's cabin which has a headroom of only 5ft or so.

The first year passed successfully, with the Dornier proving extremely reliable with few delays caused by technical troubles. Ten sectors were flown every weekday, each of about 50min duration. Maintenance was carried out at weekends by Stansted-based Inflite, with day-to-day checks performed by Suckling. At one point the airline considered the operation of flights to Jersey at weekends, but these and the long-awaited Rotterdam link were never started. Unfortunately, the airline began to suffer difficulties at its home base during early 1988 when the normally well-drained grass surface at Ipswich became waterlogged. It brought a ban on the use of the 228, forcing the company to transfer its operations to Stansted for a time with a resultant long coach trip for passengers and expense for the airline. Negotiations with nearby Wattisham brought permission to use the military facilities while the grass dried out at Ipswich and the numerous ruts and holes repaired. There was of course only one sensible solution which entailed the provision of a hard runway, but this was highly unlikely to be approved by the airport's owner.

In June, Suckling was once more forced to move, this time because the Wattisham runway was to be resurfaced. After another short spell at Stansted, a permanent base was urgently sought with the choice resting largely with Cambridge and Norwich. While the latter authorities were keen to accommodate the unfortunate company, Suckling considered the competition from the resident Air UK would be a major disadvantage. So with Cambridge thought to be the better alternative, approaches were made to the owner of the relatively quiet airfield. As a result, from 18 July 1988 the Dornier 228 began its duties from a new home, flying slightly modified schedules to both Manchester and Amsterdam. While it meant a road journey for the Ipswich passengers, it was no quicker to travel to Norwich or Stansted so the airline did not lose all of its loyal support. In any case there was a considerable amount of traffic between Cambridge and the Netherlands which soon came to appreciate Suckling's services.

During the next 10 years the airline continued to fly the Dutch services from Cambridge and also expanded its Manchester operation to include a link between the northwest airport and Amsterdam for a time. However, it also took over the Luton-Paris run from CityFlyer for which purpose the airline introduced a Dornier 328, once again pioneering a new type on the UK register. In due course the French sector was extended to Norwich, the latter also becoming the East Anglian terminal for the Manchester schedules in place of Cambridge. At the end of October 1996 the carrier took over the Stansted-Rotterdam route, but this was soon dropped from the network. On the other hand a twice-daily Do228 link between Norwich and Edinburgh was started after Air UK ended its long-established Scottish link following a spate of reorganisation. In late 1996 this also produced a franchise-style agreement with Suckling for the latter to operate the Stansted-Zürich thrice-daily services with a second Do328. When the Swiss city was dropped from Air UK's network in January 1998, Suckling's Dornier was transferred to Southampton where it began three daily visits to Amsterdam under a codesharing agreement with KLM uk.

FLEET:

Regn	Series	C/n
Dornier Do228		
G-BMMR	200	8063
G-BUXT	202K	8065
G-BVPT	202K	8165
G-BVTZ	202K	8157
Dornier Do328		
G-BWIR	110	3023
G-BWWT	110	3022

Titan Airways (AWC)

Head Office: Enterprise House, Stansted Airport, Essex CM24 1QW
Tel: (01279) 680616 Fax: (01279) 680110

The airline began operations in 1988 with one Cessna 404 for use on ad hoc passenger and freight charters. This activity has steadily been expanded by the company until Titan now operates throughout the UK, Europe, North Africa and the Middle East. Another of its activities includes back-up for other carriers either short of capacity or suffering technical delays, for which purpose two BAe 146s are now on strength. In the early 1990s the airline operated a number of Short SD3-30s and SD3-60s, but these have now been reduced until only one of the latter species remains in the fleet. The carrier is one of a number operating mail flights on weeknights for the Post Office, for which purpose an ATR-42 serves Inverness, Edinburgh and Stansted. Another of the breed operates Stansted-Leeds/Bradford-Liverpool-Stansted followed by a freight run to and from Düsseldorf, while an SD3-60 is dedicated to the Norwich-East Midlands-Liverpool-Norwich operation. During the summer months both the ATR-42s and SD3-60 operate in passenger configuration at weekends to ferry travellers between Jersey and regional airports such as Manston, Stansted, Gloucestershire, Birmingham and Southend.

FLEET:

Regn	Series	C/n
Aérospatiale ATR-42		
G-BUPS	300	109
G-ZAPJ	300	113
BAe 146		
G-ZAPK	200QC	E2148
G-ZAPL	200	E2030
Ce500 Citation		
G-ZAPI	-	0404
Short SD3-60		
G-ZAPD	300	SH3741

Above:
G-BUPS — Aérospatiale ATR-42-300 of Titan Airways.

Above:
G-ZAPD — Short SD3-60 Variant 100 of Titan Airways.

TNT International (NTR)
Head office: Archway House, 114-116 St Leonards Road, Windsor, Berkshire SL4 3DG
Tel: (01753) 842168   Fax: (01753) 858158

Although TNT is now a familiar sight in Europe, the company has its origins in Australia where it was founded as Thomas Nationwide Transport in 1946. Thereafter a significant role was played in the development of the air freight industry before becoming a public company in 1961. It was not until 1978 that the decision was taken to enter the European market, achieved mainly by the acquisition of existing organisations. Once established, the company began to expand its business with the purchase of the Australian IPEC Courier Group's European division, together with the freight carrier SkyPak in 1983. As a result, TNT became very active throughout the UK and the near Continent, although at this stage the operations were carried out by a road transport system, a situation destined to change in 1987.

Early in the year it was announced that an air network was to be set up, in the process giving TNT the distinction of becoming the launch customer for the new BAe 146QT (Quiet Trader) version of the four-engined airliner. Unfortunately, as an Australian company, TNT had no ability to function as an airline, especially with the rigid traffic rights situation at that time. This problem was overcome by contracting the work to carriers that possessed the necessary authority to operate over the proposed routes. Accordingly, applications were considered from four companies, with Luton-based Air Foyle emerging as the winner in readiness for the start of the initial programme. Following the delivery of the first 146, the inaugural sortie on behalf of TNT was flown on 5 May 1987 between Prestwick and Nuremburg, the

Above:
G-TNTM — BAe 146-300QT of TNT Worldwide.

Above:
OY-SEY — Boeing 727-224F of Sterling European/TNT Worldwide.

Above:
G-TNTG — BAe 146-300QT of TNT Worldwide.

German airport chosen as the hub for the European operation.

Expansion continued throughout 1988 which included the takeover of the small carrier XP Parcels, but more significantly the central hub was moved to more spacious and conveniently located accommodation at Cologne/Bonn. This was subsequently followed by a rebranding exercise in 1991 when all of the company's international elements adopted the TNT Express Worldwide identity. During the next year, half-ownership of the latter was sold to GD Net, a company consisting of five postal authorities in Canada, France, Germany, the Netherlands and Sweden.

A new owner took over in 1996 when it was revealed that TNT had been acquired by the Dutch postal and telecommunications corporation known as KPN. There were no major changes of policy resulting from the transaction, although a statement was issued confirming that the group would continue to be very strongly focused on Europe. This commitment was evident in March 1998 with the move of TNT's main hub to Liège in Belgium, where custom-built premises have replaced the facilities at Cologne. The move was necessary because of runway slot availability, shortage of apron space and the lack of an expansion area to relieve the increasing congestion.

TNT employs 17 BAe 146QTs for its operations, eight based in the UK and flown by Air Foyle, two in Germany with Eurowings, two are operated by the Italian company Mistral Air, while the remaining five are flown by Pan Air in Spain. In addition TNT uses several other types including a pair of Metros, Short 330/360s and a LET-410, all of which carry loose freight. Such was the demand in 1994 that TNT decided to introduce its first hush kitted Boeing 727-200 flown by Hunting Cargo Airlines (Ireland). Its 23-tonne payload has subsequently proved invaluable and has resulted in others joining the fleet, all examples of the type now being operated by Sterling European. Plans are being made for the introduction of the Airbus A300B4 during 1998, with up to 14 of the wide-bodied freighters likely to be acquired eventually.

Although an extensive schedule is flown five nights per week, utilisation of the aircraft is low, with each flying an average of four 1hr sectors. This may not be practical with the larger type, which could be better suited to two stages carrying high volume loads. Airports served in the UK are currently Belfast, Coventry, Edinburgh, Liverpool and Stansted, all being linked via the hub to some 37 European destinations.

FLEET:

Regn	Series	C/n
BAe 146		
D-ADEI	200QT	E2086
D-ANTJ	200QT	E2100
EC-ELT	200QT	E2102
EC-EPA	200QT	E2089
EC-FFY	300QT	E3154
EC-FVY	200QT	E2117
EC-FZE	200QT	E2105
G-TJPM	300QT	E3150
G-TNTA	200QT	E2056
G-TNTB	200QT	E2067
G-TNTE	300QT	E3153
G-TNTG	300QT	E3182
G-TNTK	300QT	E3186
G-TNTL	300QT	E3168
G-TNTM	300QT	E3166
G-TNTR	300QT	E3151
I-TNTC	200QT	E2078
Boeing 727		
OY-SET	227F	21245
OY-SEU	243F	21269
OY-SEV	281F	20571
OY-SEW	287F	21688
OY-SEY	224F	20659
OY-TNT	281F	20725

Virgin Atlantic Airways
(VS/VIR)
Head Office: The Office, Crawley Business Quarter, Manor Royal, Crawley, West Sussex RH10 2NU
Tel: (01293) 562345   Fax: (01293) 561721

In 1982 British Atlantic Airways was formed to operate high quality passenger services to link London and New York. During the course of the lengthy preparations for a start-up in 1984, the company was acquired by the Virgin Record Group, with the consequence that the name was changed to Virgin Atlantic Airways. A different policy was pursued by the new management which meant that the flights would be aimed at a wider range of travellers by offering lower fares. The inaugural service was flown by a Boeing 747 between Gatwick and New York (Newark) on 22 June 1984, to be quickly accepted by the travelling public as a worthy competitor for BA. In the early days the airline arranged for feeder services to ferry passengers from Maastricht in the Netherlands to Gatwick, but although good loads were obtained for the leased Viscount, few of the passengers actually continued to the US. Since sufficient traffic was generated in the UK, the Dutch connection was dropped. Virgin later managed to gain access to Heathrow for some of its departures, routes now including Johannesburg, Hong Kong, Los Angeles, Miami, New York (Newark and JFK), San Francisco, Tokyo and Washington DC. Gatwick has not been abandoned by any means since the airport handles flights to Boston, New York (Newark) and Orlando, the frequency of the Florida service becoming twice-daily in July 1998. The airline introduced regular sorties to Orlando from Manchester in May 1996 with a Boeing 767 leased from Martinair, but the operation is now normally maintained by an Airbus A340. In addition to its long-haul activities, Virgin also provides a regular link with Athens from both Gatwick and Heathrow using a solitary A320.

The airline took delivery of its eighth A340 and fifth Boeing 747-400 during 1997 to add to its collection of earlier 747 variants. In the future Virgin will be taking delivery of eight examples of the A340-600, the stretched version of the Airbus machine, for which options are held for a similar number. When in service in 2002 the aircraft will be equipped with a number of unusual features for

Above:
G-VBUS — Airbus A340-311 of Virgin Atlantic Airways.

Above:
G-OUZO — Airbus A320-231 of Virgin Atlantic Airways.

Below:
G-VBIG — Boeing 747-4Q8 of Virgin Atlantic Airways.

Above:
G-VOYG — Boeing 747-283B of Virgin Atlantic Airways.

premium fare customers, such as double beds in private rooms located on the forward lower deck. It is also planned that a pub/lounge will be provided, together with an exercise and massage area complete with showers on the rear lower deck. Surprisingly, the idea for such schemes is not new, but few have ever materialised.

Virgin has now established a transatlantic alliance with Continental Airlines, replacing a similar agreement with Delta. Code-sharing was arranged to start in February 1998 to cover Virgin's US routes and its partner's Newark-Gatwick service. The arrangement will give the UK carrier access to Continental's considerable route network radiating from New York.

FLEET:

Regn	Series	C/n
Airbus A320		
G-OUZO	231	449
Airbus A340		
G-VAEL	311	015
G-VAIR	311	164
G-VBUS	311	013
G-VFLY	311	058
G-VHOL	311	002
G-VSEA	311	003
G-VSKY	311	016
G-VSUN	313	114

Boeing 747		
G-VAST	41R	28757
G-VBIG	4Q8	26255
G-VFAB	4Q8	24958
G-VGIN	243B	19732
G-VHOT	4Q8	26326
G-VIRG	287B	21189
G-VJFK	238B	20842
G-VLAX	238B	20921
G-VMIA	123	20108
G-VOYG	283B	20121
G-VTOP	4Q8	28194

For all your transport requirements, visit the Ian Allan Bookshops in Birmingham, Manchester or London.

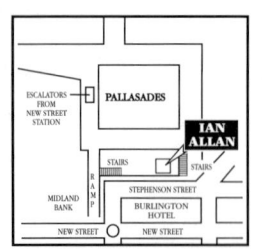

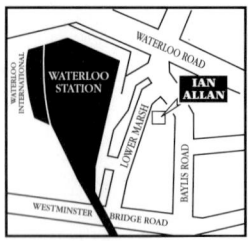

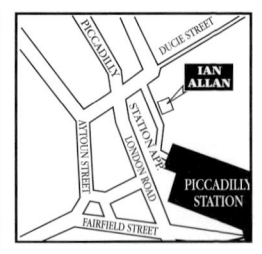

BIRMINGHAM

Unit 84
47 Stephenson Street
Birmingham B2 4DH
Tel: 0121 643 2496
Fax: 0121 643 6855

LONDON

45/46 Lower Marsh
Waterloo
London SE1 7SG
Tel: 0171 401 2100

MANCHESTER

Unit 5
Piccadilly Station Approach
Manchester M1 2GH
Tel: 0161 237 9840
Fax: 0161 237 9921

Each shop stocks a comprehensive range of books, magazines, videos, models, badges, postcards, calendars and much more!

For the full range of Ian Allan products plus books and videos from specialist publishers large and small - call into an Ian Allan Bookshop TODAY!

The Ian Allan Bookshops also offer a mail order service - please call for details.

To find out if an Ian Allan Bookshop is opening near you, please telephone: **0161 237 9840.**

IAN ALLAN *Bookshops*